DH 2
vs
ALBATROS D I/D II

Western Front 1916

JAMES F. MILLER

First published in Great Britain in 2012 by Osprey Publishing,
Midland House, West Way, Botley, Oxford, OX2 0PH, UK
44-02 23rd Street, Suite 219, Long Island City, NY 11101, USA
E-mail: info@ospreypublishing.com

OSPREY PUBLISHING IS PART OF THE OSPREY GROUP

A CIP catalogue record for this book is available from the British Library

Print ISBN: 978 1 84908 704 9
PDF ebook ISBN: 978 1 84908 705 6
ePub ebook ISBN: 978 1 78096 420 1

Edited by Tony Holmes
Cover artworks, cockpits, gunsights and armament scrap views by
Jim Laurier
Battlescene by Mark Postlethwaite
Three-views by James F. Miller
Page layout by Ken Vail Graphic Design, Cambridge, UK
Index by Alan Thatcher
Typeset in AGaramond
Map and diagrams by Bounford.com
Originated by PDQ Digital Media Solutions, Suffolk, UK
Printed in China through Bookbuilders

12 13 14 15 16   10 9 8 7 6 5 4 3 2 1

Osprey Publishing is supporting the Woodland Trust, the UK's leading
woodland conservation charity, by funding the dedication of trees.

www.ospreypublishing.com

German ranks	French ranks	USAS ranks	RFC/RAF ranks
Rittmeister (Rittm)	Cavalry Captain	Cavalry Captain	Cavalry Captain
Hauptmann (Hptm)	Capitaine	Captain	Army Captain
Oberleutnant (Oblt)	Lieutenant	First Lieutenant	Lieutenant
Leutnant (Ltn)	Sous-Lieutenant	Second Lieutenant	Second Lieutenant
Offizierstellvertreter (OffzSt)	Adjutant	Warrant Officer	Warrant Officer
Feldwebel (Fw)	Sergent-Chef	Master Sergeant	Master Sergeant
Vizefeldwebel (Vzfw)	Maréchal-des-Logis	Sergeant 1st Class	Sergeant 1st Class
Sergeant	Sergent	Sergeant	Sergeant
Unteroffizier (Uffz)	Caporal	Corporal	Corporal
Gefreiter (Gfr)	Brigadier	Private 1st Class	Private 1st Class
Flieger (Flgr)	Soldat	Private	Private

Editor's Note

For ease of comparison between types, imperial measurements are used
almost exclusively throughout this book. The exception is weapon calibres,
which are given in their official designation, whether metric or imperial.
The following data will help in converting between imperial and metric
measurements:

1 mile = 1.6km
1lb = 0.45kg
1yd = 0.9m
1ft = 0.3m
1in = 2.54cm/25.4mm
1 gallon (UK) = 4.55l
1 ton (UK) = 1.02 tonnes
1hp = 0.74kW

Acknowledgements

The author wishes to thank the following for their selfless contributions –
Dan-San Abbott, Lance Bronnenkant, Gene Buckmaster, Chris and
Charyn Cordry, Tom and Karen Dillon, Russ Gannon, Barry Gray, Jon
Guttman, Bert Hughlett, Reinhard Kastner, Peter Kilduff, Herb and Sarah
Kilmer, Stephen Lawson, League of World War One Historians, James G.
and Judy Miller, Jim, Major and LaFonda Miller, Naples Fitness Boot
Camp, Alex Revell, Marton Szigeti, Manfred Thiemeyer, Greg
VanWyngarden, Aaron Weaver and Reinhard Zankl. Title-page photograph
courtesy Aaron Weaver; unless otherwise credited, all photographs are from
the author's collection.

DH 2 cover art

No. 24 Sqn's Capt John Andrews and 2Lt Kelvin Crawford look on as
the stricken Albatros D II of *Jasta 2 Staffelführer* and 11-victory ace
Stefan Kirmaier begins its final descent near Les Boeufs, in France, on
22 November 1916. Andrews later recalled that moments before 'several
Hostile Aircraft [HA] had dived' at he and Crawford, but they did not
attack, allowing him to gain advantage on the lowest machine and fire ten
rounds that caused the Albatros to fall out of control. Crawford had also
attacked Kirmaier, firing a half drum until the D II 'nose dived'. Kirmaier
was fatally wounded, his smoking Albatros diving away at a shallow angle
until it hit terra firma, the force of the crash burying the scout's engine
beneath the ground. Both No. 24 Sqn pilots shared credit for the victory,
which was Andrews' seventh and Crawford's second success. (Artwork by
Jim Laurier)

Albatros D II cover art

The day after Kirmaier's loss, de facto *Jasta 2 Staffelführer* Ltn Manfred von
Richthofen led the unit's Albatros D Is and D IIs in a diving attack against
three No. 24 Sqn DH 2s near Bapaume, in France. A 'violent fight' ensued,
during which Kirmaier's victor John Andrews had his DH 2 'badly shot
about' and von Richthofen and No. 24 Sqn commander Maj Lanoe
Hawker entered a turning dogfight that is now legendary. Unable to gain
a firing position on von Richthofen while drifting further behind German
lines, Hawker was forced to make a break for friendly territory. Although
his DH 2 could not outrun a new Albatros D II, Hawker's jinking nearly
allowed him to reach the lines, but he was struck in the head and killed by
the gunfire of his tenacious foe, crashing near Ligny-Thilloy, in France.
(Artwork by Jim Laurier)

CONTENTS

INTRODUCTION

While modern air forces employ time-tested, combat-proven tactics and decades-old aeroplanes designed on well understood aeronautical principles and built with ample time for testing and refining, air forces of World War I were literally writing the book on tactics and aeroplane design as dictated by the current state of the war. Indeed, throughout the conflict a perpetual reactionary arms race existed to counter and hopefully conquer the enemy's latest aeroplane technology. Nowhere was this more evident than with single-seat scouts.

Better known today as 'fighter aeroplanes', single-seat scouts were born as a direct result of two-seater aerial reconnaissance and artillery observation. Such infantry cooperation aeroplanes were crucial for the furtherance of army strategic and tactical planning for ground force success. This was particularly the case on the static Western Front, where trench-based warfare throttled any cavalry-based reconnaissance. Without exaggeration, two-seater photographic reconnaissance was as important in World War I as satellites are today.

Naturally, it became desirable for all combatants not only to amass as much intelligence as possible via two-seater excursions over the frontlines but to simultaneously prevent the enemy from achieving the same. This begat two-seater crews arming themselves for aerial interception of their belligerent counterparts, but soon single-seat 'scouts' were developed to use speed to dash quickly over the lines, conduct a specific observation, and then quickly regain the lines. However, both sides realised that single-seat scouts provided an effective means with which to hunt and shoot down enemy reconnaissance aeroplanes, as well as to protect their own reconnaissance types from similar treatment. A natural result of these tactical implementations was scout-versus-scout combat – the 'fighter aeroplane' and 'dogfighting' were born.

No. 24 Sqn DH 2s 6000 (left) and 5925 (right) at Bertangles in July 1916 – note 5925's slightly lower nacelle front. This aircraft was one of three DH 2s involved in an epic clash with *Jasta* 2 that saw the loss of No. 24 Sqn CO Maj Lanoe Hawker.

However, the superiority pendulum swung without equality as each side strove to counter what the enemy already possessed. The Germans struck first with their Fokker Eindeckers, armed with a single Maxim machine gun that was synchronised to fire through the propeller arc. Not necessarily an extremely nimble aeroplane – it did not have to be when pursuing sluggish two-seater reconnaissance types such as the Royal Aircraft Factory (RAF) BE 2c – the monoplane's armament and speed (approximately 88mph compared to the BE 2c's modest 69mph at 10,000ft) allowed it to plunder Allied reconnaissance machines. This in turn gave rise to the legendary 'Fokker Scourge' description given to German air superiority over the Western Front from late 1915 through to early 1916.

As yet the Triple Entente (Great Britain, France and Russia) had no reliable synchronisation gear with which to counter the new threat. However, the single-seat French Nieuport 11 'Bebe' soon appeared with a single Lewis machine gun mounted atop the upper wing that fired *over* the propeller arc, bypassing the need for propeller synchronisation.

The British answer to the problem was to employ the 'pusher' aeroplane concept – i.e. locate the engine behind the cockpit to allow the pilot freedom to fire a machine gun forward without any interference from the propeller. This arrangement had previously been used in two-seaters such as the Farman F 40 and RAF FE 2b, but the Aircraft Manufacturing Company's DH 2 was the first single-seat pusher designed specifically for air-to-air interdiction.

Now equipped with fighters that were as fast and more nimble than the German monoplanes and, crucially, available in greater numbers, the Entente had once again

With a dose of right rudder, *Jasta* 2's Ltn Otto Höhne guns Albatros D I 390/16 *Hö* on its takeoff run in the autumn of 1916. Höhne had shot down six aeroplanes with *Jasta* 2 by the time he was wounded in January 1917. A year later he would return to the unit as *Staffelführer*.

achieved control of the skies over the Western Front by the summer of 1916. A post-war German analysis concluded:

> The start of the Somme battle [1 July 1916] unfortunately coincided with the low point in the technical development of our aircraft. The unquestioned air supremacy we had enjoyed in early 1916 by virtue of our Fokker monoplane fighters had shifted over to the enemy's Nieuport, Vickers [generic German term for British lattice-tailed pushers, in this instance referring to the DH 2] and Sopwith aircraft in March and April.

As the German monoplanes were replaced by biplane fighters such as the Fokker D I and various Halberstadt machines, pilots wanted a fighter that had power enough to promote speed *and* bear the weight of twin-gun firepower. Enter the Albatros D I and D II, each boasting a 160hp engine that gave the pilots what they had asked for. The Albatros Ds were not as manoeuvrable as the Nieuport 11 or DH 2, but this was not a detriment when one considers that shooting down ungainly two-seaters was a primary endeavour. All pilots sought to attack under a cloak of surprise, using speed to swiftly approach one's target unseen and then hammer it down before the crew of the aeroplane was even aware that they were under attack.

Head to head, the DH 2 was more manoeuvrable than the Albatros D I and D II, but the latter were faster, had better rates of climb and were equipped with two belt-fed machine guns and 1,000 rounds of ammunition. The DH 2 had a single gun with less than half that amount of ammunition, carried in 47- or 97-round drums that had to be replaced during combat. The Albatros also enjoyed a much more reliable inline engine than the DH 2's rotary motor, which was prone to power loss or outright failure due to mechanical faults. However, even with properly running engines, speed triumphs manoeuvrability. The latter is a defensive tactic and fighter aeroplanes are offensive weapons, best employing surprise in order to prevail over an opponent. The DH 2's nimble attributes, therefore, could not easily overcome the Albatros's superior speed (the DH 2 was nearly 20mph slower in level flight), especially when in a dive, and firepower.

Royal Flying Corps (RFC) pilot Capt R. H. M. S. Saundby's recollections succinctly set the stage for the chapters that follow:

> The Albatros single-seater fighting machine was the first formidable tractor [engine in front] biplane scout produced by the enemy. While we had occasionally met them before, they only became numerous and, therefore, offensive at the beginning of November [1916]. The de Havilland Scout had a hard job when outnumbered by these machines, and only carried on because of its handiness and manoeuvring power, for its speed and climb were much inferior to these new Huns [slang for Germans and/or German aeroplanes].

This outstanding close-up photograph of American volunteer pilot Lt Geoffrey H. Bonnell of No. 32 Sqn clearly reveals the DH 2's nacelle and single 0.303in Lewis machine gun. Bonnell would later join the US Army Air Service and command the 147th Aero Squadron. (Aaron Weaver)

CHRONOLOGY

1914

March Geoffrey de Havilland joins the Aircraft Manufacturing Company as chief aeroplane designer and test pilot. Begins work on a two-seater pusher, forerunner of the DH 2.

June Albatros Type DD wins 100km (60 miles) speed prize at the Aspern *Flugmeeting* in Vienna. Designed by Ernst Heinkel and Robert Thelen, the Type DD is considered to be the forerunner of the Albatros D series of scouts.

28 June Archduke Franz Ferdinand of Austria assassinated by Serbian student Gavrilo Princip, beginning a period of international diplomatic manoeuvring.

July To end Serbian interference in Bosnia, Austria-Hungary delivers a ten-demand ultimatum to Serbia, intentionally made to be unacceptable and provoke war. Serbia agrees to eight demands.

28 July Austria-Hungary declares war on Serbia.

29 July Russian Empire orders partial mobilisation in support of Serbia.

30 July German Empire delivers ultimatum to Russia to cease mobilisation against Austria-Hungary.

1 August France orders mobilisation and Germany declares war on Russia.

3 August Germany declares war on France and invades Belgium.

4 August UK declares war on Germany in support of Belgian neutrality. World War I fully under way.

1915

June de Havilland conducts inaugural DH 2 flight and begins series of test flights and refinements.

Summer German monoplanes armed with synchronised machine guns decimate RFC reconnaissance two-seaters, begetting the 'Fokker Scourge'.

No. 32 Sqn DH 2 7907 features clear doped fabric sides, grey metal nacelle panels and dark undercarriage struts. A black ring on the white wheel cover denotes a 'B' Flight machine. (Aaron Weaver)

9 August	DH 2 prototype sent to France for combat evaluation is shot down and captured mostly intact by the Germans.

1916

February	DH 2 arrives in France with No. 24 Sqn.
June	Thelen design team's Albatros D I undergoes flight evaluation and static load tests at Adlershof.
18 June	German 15-victory ace Ltn d R Max Immelmann is killed in action, his death marking the end of the 'Fokker Scourge'.
July	Albatros D I ordered into production.
1 July	The Battle of the Somme commences. British Army suffers 60,000 killed or wounded on the first day of the offensive.
August	Germans implement the *Jagdstaffel*, a dedicated group of single-seat fighters tasked primarily with hunting enemy two-seater reconnaissance and artillery-spotting machines.
16 September	Albatros D Is and a single D II arrive in the frontline with *Jagdstaffel* 2.
28 October	*Jagdstaffel* 2 *Staffelführer* and 40-victory ace Hptm Oswald Boelcke is killed after a mid-air collision with Ltn Erwin Böhme, who survives.
22 November	No. 24 Sqn pilots Capt John Andrews and 2Lt Kelvin Crawford shoot down and kill *Jagdstaffel* 2 *Staffelführer* Stefan Kirmaier.
23 November	No. 24 Sqn commanding officer and RFC luminary Maj Lanoe Hawker is shot down and killed by *Jasta* 2's Manfred von Richthofen after an eight-minute swirling dogfight and race to the lines near Bapaume, France.
Late December	Albatros D IIIs begin arriving at frontline *Jagdstaffeln*.

DESIGN AND DEVELOPMENT

DH 2

In the first decade of the 20th century the UK's aviation endeavours lagged significantly behind those of their continental neighbours France and Germany. France had taken to the new heavier-than-air aeroplane with an ardent fervour after American Wilbur Wright so ably demonstrated the Wright Flyer there in 1908. Germany had focused its aviation interest primarily upon lighter-than-air machines, such as Graf Zeppelin's rigid airships, which by 1909 had gained acceptance into the German military.

Concurrently, the British had no aviation mindset either. Case in point, in 1908 the British Secretary of State for War's response to inquiries regarding the placement of government aeroplane manufacturing orders said, succinctly, 'we regret we cannot do this as we are trustees of the public purse and we do not consider that aeroplanes will be of any possible use for war purposes'.

However, English journalist George Holt Thomas set out to change that opinion. In 1906 he had offered a £1,000 prize for the first heavier-than-air machine to complete a straight-line flight of one mile, and his frequent trips to Paris kept him in the know regarding the significant advancements of French aviation. These trips included visits to French manufacturers and aviation pioneers, particularly Henry Farman, and after attending the 1909 Reims Aviation Meeting Holt Thomas returned to England determined to increase the country's aviation interests and awareness.

Toward that end he organised the first officially recognised British aviation meeting at Blackpool, arranged demonstration flights around London and then became manager of French aviator Louis Paulhan, who subsequently won a £10,000 prize for being the first to fly from London to Manchester.

In September 1910 Holt Thomas attended French army manoeuvres on the continent, where he witnessed the progress military aviation had made with aerial reconnaissance and artillery spotting. Recognising the aeroplane's military importance, but cognizant of the British lack of progress in its furtherance, Holt Thomas wrote a letter to the *Daily Mail* on 17 September that said, in part, 'A new weapon of the utmost importance in war has appeared, and with that weapon our Army is wholly unprovided'. Nevertheless, the British army remained unconvinced that the aeroplane would replace the cavalry as a method of reconnaissance.

Undeterred, Holt Thomas used his influences with the press to further his cause, and in October 1910 was able to arrange purchase of two French aeroplanes (a Henry Farman Type *Militaire* and a Paulhan biplane) for the War Office, and further pressure eventually resulted in the British government agreeing to a nearly 500 per cent increase in the 1911 allotment for military aviation, from £9,000 to £52,000. Shortly thereafter Holt Thomas brokered a deal with the Farman Brothers to build and sell their machines in Britain through his Aeroplane Supply Company, which he established in 1911.

When a similar attempt to broker a deal with Prince Henry of Prussia to construct Zeppelin airships fell through in 1912, Holt Thomas sought and received licence to build French Astra-Torres airships and subsequently formed Airships, Ltd. In May 1912 he merged his two companies, and the following month he re-registered them as the Aircraft Manufacturing Company (AMC – the oft-used 'Airco' prefix was not officially adopted by the Aircraft Manufacturing Company until October 1918), whose first British-built Maurice Farman machine was completed in 1913. Holt Thomas's fledgling company soon became the pinnacle of the British aircraft industry.

With a want to expand AMC beyond manufacturing and into aviation design, Holt Thomas was advised to contact a 26-year-old aircraft designer by the name of Geoffrey de Havilland. Born on 27 July 1882, de Havilland had graduated from Crystal Palace Engineering School in 1903 and had initially worked as a motor engineering draughtsman in Birmingham prior to returning to London to take up employment with a bus-building company.

Intrigued by reports of aviation feats and advancements on the continent, de Havilland and a partner quit their jobs to build an aeroplane of their own, financed by de Havilland's grandfather. They accomplished this in 1909, but the machine was destroyed after de Havilland stalled it on takeoff. Uninjured, de Havilland and his partner assembled a second machine the following year and flew it successfully. The aircraft was purchased by the War Office, who then offered de Havilland a position as

Prior to his tenure with AMC, 26-year-old Geoffrey de Havilland designed the legendary BE and FE series of aeroplanes for the Royal Aircraft Factory. Although he was initially hesitant to work on pusher designs with AMC, his efforts produced the redoubtable DH 2.

both designer and test pilot at His Majesty's Balloon Factory, forerunner of the famous Royal Aircraft Factory.

So employed, de Havilland helped design and develop such legendary aeroplanes as the BE and FE series, but by 1914 he found himself inspecting aircraft from other designers rather than working on his own. After voicing dissatisfaction about his plight, it was suggested (by the same man who had told Holt Thomas to contact de Havilland) that he seek employment with AMC as it was expanding into aircraft design. Taking heed of this advice, de Havilland approached Holt Thomas when the latter next visited the RAF facility at Farnborough, and on 23 March 1914 he signed on as AMC's chief designer and test pilot.

Initially working on a rotary-engined version of the BE 2, de Havilland was soon redirected by Holt Thomas to commence design work on a two-seater pusher biplane instead. Although de Havilland was reluctant at first because he knew the tractor configuration was more aerodynamically sound than the pusher, Holt Thomas had made the request because it was believed within the RFC that the pusher was a superior weapons platform at the time. With the engine and propeller behind the pilot, the new scout could dispense with the then oft-unreliable interrupter gear needed to enable a machine gun to fire through a propeller arc.

With experience from working on previous pusher designs, de Havilland set about creating the DH 1. A two-seater powered by a 70hp Renault V8 engine, the aircraft was armed with a telescopically mounted Lewis machine gun that could be fired by the observer in the front cockpit.

The war with Germany that everybody had expected finally broke out that August, and as a member of the RFC reserve, de Havilland was ordered to report to Montrose, in Scotland, where he flew anti-submarine sorties over the Firth of Forth. Fortunately, then RFC Military Wing commandant Lt Col Hugh Trenchard (future Brigadier-General and Officer Commanding the RFC in France) soon realised de Havilland would better serve his country as a test pilot and sent him back to Farnborough. Holt Thomas also lobbied for de Havilland's return, and after three

An AMC DH 1A, forerunner of the DH 2, seen here in service with No. 14 Sqn in the Middle East. DH 1As were DH 1s fitted with a 120hp inline Beardmore engine, which generated a top speed of 90mph at sea level. (Aaron Weaver)

DH 2

25ft 2.5in

9ft 7in

28ft 3in

months he successfully managed to have his chief designer seconded back to AMC in December 1914, whereupon he returned to work on the DH 1. The prototype was completed in February 1915, but by then the RFC favoured use of the RAF's FE 2a, which carried a larger payload than the DH 1.

de Havilland worked on several concurrent designs, but in March he and his design team of Charles Walker and Howard Ker concentrated on a single-seat pusher biplane – born from a scaled-down version of the DH 1 – which soon became known as the DH 2. The biplane design sandwiched a streamlined wood and metal nacelle that held the pilot, fuel tank and 100hp Gnome Monosoupape rotary engine, with twin booms leading back to the empennage. de Havilland made the inaugural flight in the aircraft on 1 June 1915 and reported that the machine was tail heavy, but after employing some weight-saving measures and moving the nacelle forward 4in the craft flew satisfactorily two weeks later with a top speed of 88mph at 6,000ft. The chosen armament was a single Lewis 0.303in machine gun that was externally mounted to port within an aluminium fairing, and this could be elevated by the pilot.

On 22 June the prototype was evaluated by Capt Robert Maxwell Pike, who suggested installing streamlined flying wires to increase speed and angling the vertical stabiliser to starboard to counter engine torque. Overall, Pike thought the DH 2's visibility was the best of any aeroplane he had ever flown, and that he 'has not seen a German machine which can equal this Scout for speed and climbing power'. Following alterations, the prototype was assigned serial number 4732 and in late July it was sent to France for in-service evaluation with the RFC's No. 5 Sqn. Unfortunately, on 9 August Pike was mortally wounded by a German two-seater observer, but before dying he crash-landed behind enemy lines, giving the Germans a mostly intact and up-close preview of their new adversary.

Regardless of the loss, AMC conducted further alterations to its design, the most notable of which was moving the Lewis gun from its external mount and relocating it within

A factory photograph of the first production batch DH 2 5943, equipped with a two-bladed propeller and gravity tank mounted under the upper port wing. (Aaron Weaver)

the cockpit atop a central mounting bracket. The first production batch was ordered in September 1915, and these machines (DH 2s 5916 to 6015) began appearing that November. Subsequent 100-machine production batches were ordered in March 1916 (7842 to 7941) and August 1916 (A2533 to A2632). A 50-aircraft production order was placed in October 1916 (A4764 to A4813) and a final 100 machines (A4988 to A5087) were ordered in September 1916. Changes during these production orders included replacing the two-bladed propeller with one of four blades, relocating the gravity fuel tank from the upper wing's undersurface to its uppersurface, enlargement of the ailerons, employing a balanced rudder and various changes with the layout of the cockpit instrumentation.

The first DH 2s arrived at the Central Flying School in December 1915 and four were sent to Nos 5, 11 and 18 Sqns in France for evaluation in early 1916. The machine arrived in France in earnest with No. 24 Sqn in February 1916, and by late May Nos 29 and 32 Sqns had been equipped with DH 2s. 1916 saw 222 DH 2s serve with the British Expeditionary Force (BEF) in France. DH 2s also saw combat with the Middle East Brigade but in comparatively smaller numbers – a single machine was delivered in 1916 and only 31 in all of 1917. Home Defence also received two machines in 1917, but none thereafter. 1916 was unquestionably the DH 2's year, initially dominating the skies but subsequently enduring a hard fought fall from grace.

ALBATROS D I/II

For much of the first decade of the 20th century Germany's aviation aspirations focused on lighter- rather than heavier-than-air flight. Having formed a *Luftschiffer Detachement* (Lighter-than-air Detail) in 1884 to evaluate the reconnaissance applications of balloons, by 1901 the *Detachement* had grown into a *Luftschiffer Bataillon* (Lighter-than-air Battalion) that employed free and moored balloons. In 1900 the first practical powered flight of a lighter-than-air machine occurred via a 17-minute flight of Graf Zeppelin's rigid airship LZ 1, and this event piqued *Kriegsministerium* (War Ministry) interest in the craft's possible military usefulness.

Still, new heavier-than-air machines were not unknown. In 1905 the Americans Orville and Wilbur Wright brought their aeroplane to Europe to demonstrate controlled powered flight and showed its practicality via a flight of 39km (24 miles). Nevertheless, the War Ministry conference of 1906 established that military aeronautics ought to focus on rigid airships, in large part due to their familiarity with lighter-than-air machines versus the newer heavier-than-air craft.

However, 1909 saw a boon in the interest and development of the aeroplane thanks to an injection of public money to promote development. Demonstration flights were conducted and the country's first flight meeting took place at the inaugural German aerodrome at Johannisthal, near Berlin. Various manufacturers attended this event and, under licence, began building aeroplanes of foreign design. In October of that year a 3km (1.8-mile) flight from Johannisthal netted the pilot a 40,000-mark prize for the first flight of a German aeroplane powered by a German aero engine. Lighter-than-air machines still retained the focus of the German military, but many people realised that the aeroplane was coming of age.

One such person was German biologist Dr Walther Huth, who so embraced the thought of flight via aeroplane that he sent his chauffeur Simon Brunnhuber to France and paid for his flight training there. Upon successfully completing his tuition, Brunnhuber returned with a Levasseur Antoinette single-seat monoplane that Huth had purchased. Later, he also bought a Farman two-seater. With foresight enough to recognise the aeroplane's future importance toward military applications, Huth contacted the *Kriegsministerium* in October 1909 and offered the services of his aeroplanes for the purpose of flight instruction, *gratis*, with Brunnhuber serving as instructor. While the subsequent negotiations were underway Huth established his own company – the Albatros Flugzeugwerke GmbH, named after the seabird with which he was familiar from his scientific studies – at Johannisthal that December.

Negotiations with the *Militärbehörde* (Military Authority) lasted until March 1910, when Huth's proposal was accepted. It is believed flight instruction began that July, and by March 1911 Brunnhuber had trained six pilots. Progress had been slow due to a lack of funds, suitable training space (aero engines frightened the horses of troops training nearby) and lingering doubts regarding the aeroplane's useful military role. There were also concerns about the long training times for aeroplane maintenance personnel. Regardless, training continued as Albatros was contracted to build lattice-framed Farman reproductions with the type designation Albatros MZ 2.

In 1912 Albatros hired *Diplom-Ingenieur* (Engineering Graduate) Robert Thelen as chief designer. The 28-year-old Thelen had been the ninth German pilot trained to fly (in May 1910), and prior to joining Albatros he had been a competition pilot flying Wright biplanes. Teaming up with *Dipl. Ing.* Helmut Hirth (trained in March 1911) and employing the perfected semi-monocoque wooden fuselage designs of *Ober-Ingenieur* Hugo Grohmann, Thelen's designs moved away from the Farman type open-lattice construction. His construction technique provided enough strength via the external skin to eliminate the need for internal bracing, thereby reducing weight and increasing performance and payload capacity. Albatros would soon become renowned for building aeroplanes with enclosed wooden fuselages (*Rumpf-Doppeldecker*, or fuselage double-decker).

Chief among these would be the Albatros Type DD, later known as the B I, designed in early 1913 by Ernst Heinkel (whose future company produced many aeroplanes in World War II) and improved by Thelen's suggestions based on his experience as a pilot. Thelen referred to the type as 'Albatros DD, system Heinkel-Thelen'. Powered by a 100hp Mercedes D I engine, the semi-monocoque three-bay (*Dreistielig*) DD was a successful design that in the months immediately prior to World War I set several world records for duration and altitude. That summer a single-bay version known as the *Renndoppeldecker*, which was powered by a 100hp Hiero engine, won the 100km (60 miles) speed prize at the Aspern *Flugmeeting* in Vienna. Experience gained with this machine is considered to have sown the seeds for the future Albatros D I.

Following the commencement of World War I in August 1914 Albatros concentrated on manufacturing two-seat B- and C-type machines. Aerial observation and artillery spotting were crucial for the support of ground forces, which required that these types had manufacturing and engine allocation priority. Naturally, as the war progressed the opposing forces developed single-seat fighters to protect their two-seater observation machines and destroy those of the enemy.

These fighters were, in the main, powered by rotary engines. Those powered by inline motors had been somewhat hamstrung by the lack of availability of higher horsepower engines, as they were prioritised for B- and C-type machines. This did not lessen the born-from-experience calls from fighter pilots requesting that single-engined machines be equipped with higher horsepower motors and armed with two rather than the then-standard single machine gun.

Thoughts also surfaced among German pilots that while rotary-engined fighters – with their rapid capacity for engine start and takeoff – were ideal for intercepting enemy machines, a fighter powered by a more reliable inline engine and armed with twin machine guns would be better suited to protecting two-seater aeroplanes beyond the enemy lines. Although German aerial tactics evolved differently, this mindset came at a time of increasing engine manufacture productivity, and it set the stage for the birth of a new breed of fighter – and none too soon.

German aerial domination, once achieved by rotary-engined Fokker and Pfalz E-type wing-warping monoplanes, had been lost to the more nimble French Nieuport 11s and British DH 2s, which not only out-flew the German fighters but were present in greater numbers. Rather than compete with the manoeuvrability of these adversaries, the Thelen-led Albatros design bureau set to work on what became the Albatros D I and D II. By April 1916, the bureau had developed a sleek yet rugged machine that featured the usual Albatros semi-monocoque wooden construction and

Robert Thelen was a 28-year-old pilot when he joined the *Albatros Werke GmbH* in 1912 as Chief Designer. His design team ultimately begat the Albatros D lineage that was so crucial to the success of the German mid-war effort. Thelen died in 1968. (Collection DEHLA)

ALBATROS D II

24ft 3in

8ft 8in

27ft 11in

employed a 160hp Mercedes D III engine with power enough to allow the aeroplane to be equipped with two forward-firing machine guns. Visual hallmarks of the D I and early-production D II included fuselage-mounted Windhoff radiators and matching chords for the upper and lower wings.

On 6 June 1916 a D I prototype began flight evaluation and static-load testing at the Adlershof test centre. Results were mixed. A test flight yielded a climb rate of 1,000m (3,280ft) in four minutes, 2,000m (6,560ft) in eight minutes, 3,000m (9,840ft) in 14 minutes and 4,000m (13,120ft) in 22 minutes – a good performance even when considering that the machine was unarmed and thus lighter than gross weight. Yet in further static load tests the D I's upper wing rear spar failed the load requirements for pulling out of a dive, and when retested on 3 July it failed again. Tests for gliding flight and inverted flight requirements were passed on 4 and 5 July, and two days later a new wing spar was tested, which finally passed as well.

Meanwhile, *Idflieg* (*Inspektion der Fliegertruppen*, or Inspectorate of Aviation Troops) had ordered 12 pre-production machines – D.380/16 to 391/16 – of which several were armed and sent forward for combat evaluation. By July the *Zentral Abnahme Kommision* (*ZAK*, or Central Acceptance Commission) recommended the Albatros D I for production, after which *Idflieg* signed an order for 100 Albatros fighters.

However, concurrent with the development of the D I, Thelen's team had also designed and constructed a second machine that was similar to the D I, the Albatros D II. It is important to note that these aircraft evolved simultaneously, and that the D II was not the result of post-combat feedback from D I pilots. Proof is found not only in photographs but in the pre-production order of 12 machines. One of the latter was D II D.386/16 (which became legendary German ace Oswald Boelcke's machine, as will be seen), and another example (D.388/16) served as a prototype Albatros D III.

Essentially, the D I and D II were the same machine, but the latter had several noticeable external differences and improvements. For example, the D I's inverted V-strut centre section pylon was replaced by outwardly splayed N-struts in the D II, this arrangement improving forward visibility. The wing gap was reduced by lowering

OPPOSITE
Built by Albatros at Johannisthal, D.1724/16 was a third production batch machine and one of the last D IIs to employ the fuselage-mounted Windhoff radiators, which were replaced by a Teeves und Braun radiator centrally located in the upper wing (as seen just three machines later, on D.1727/16). Flown by *Kasta* 11 pilot Ltn Karl Emil Schaefer – who went on to fly D IIIs with *Jasta* 11 and down a total of 30 aeroplanes, winning the Orden Pour le Mérite before being killed on 5 June 1917 – D.1724/16 represents a typical D II, with camouflaged wings and large national markings on a glossy wood fuselage. The large serial number on the vertical stabiliser is a hallmark of Johannisthal-built machines, although soon such simple personal markings as a bordered circle would give way to more ostentatiously decorated aeroplanes.

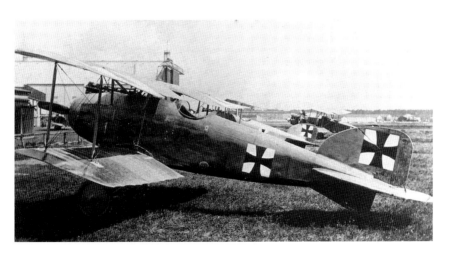

Recent photographic analysis has revealed this pre-production Albatros D II – shown here next to a pre-production D I at Johannisthal, circa summer 1916 – was received by *Jasta* 2 in September and became Oswald Boelcke's D.386/16. The nearby D I is also believed to have reached *Jasta* 2 and been flown by Ltn Dieter Collin, who shot down two No. 24 Sqn DH 2s during November and December. (Aaron Weaver)

19

The Albatros D I prototype at Johannisthal. Noteworthy items that were changed prior to production include the upturned exhaust manifold, unbalanced elevator and externally routed rudder cables. (Greg VanWyngarden)

the upper wing by 250mm (9.8in), which also improved forward and upper visibility. Finally, the side-mounted Windhoff radiators were replaced with a Teeves und Braun wing-mounted radiator located between the new struts. This modification did not take effect until after the first production run of 50 D IIs (excluding Boelcke's pre-production D II D.386/16, which was built with a wing-mounted radiator), which made up the second half of *Idflieg's* initial order for 100 Albatros fighters – 50 D Is, serialled 422 to 471/16, and 50 D IIs, 472 to 521/16 – had been completed.

In August, 50 more D IIs (890 to 939/16) were ordered from Huth's *Ostdeutsche Albatros Werke* (OAW, an independent firm at the time that would be assimilated into the main Albatros company in October 1917), located in Schneidmühl. Designated the Albatros D II (OAW), the aircraft were constructed nearly identically to those built at Johannisthal, as were the 75 machines (1024 to 1098/16) to be built under licence by LVG (*Luftverkehrsgesellschaft*), also ordered in August. September saw Albatros receive the final D II production order for 100 machines (1700 to 1799/16), after which the focus of production shifted to the next generation of Albatros fighters, the D III (see *Duel 36 – SPAD VII vs Albatros D III* for details).

Excluding prototypes, Albatros, OAW and LVG built a total of 50 Albatros D Is and 275 Albatros D IIs. After their introduction to frontline service in early September 1916, the D I's frontline inventory peaked at 50 in October and then dwindled slowly. By the end of 1917 there were eight still in service. The D IIs enjoyed a longer service career due to their greater production numbers, peaking at more than 200 in December 1916 and sustaining this figure through to late February 1917. However, after maintaining approximately three-quarters of this number through to the end of April, the frontline inventory fell dramatically to six by year end.

TECHNICAL SPECIFICATIONS

DH 2

The AMC DH 2 arose from the need for a fast single-seat aeroplane armed with a forward-firing machine gun at a time when the still unreliable synchronisation gear necessitated that such a machine be of pusher design – i.e. engine at the rear. The standard engine used by the DH 2 was the 100hp Gnome Monosoupape 9 Type B-2, a normally aspirated, air-cooled, nine cylinder rotary motor. Fuel and oil tanks (20.8 and 4.5 gallons, respectively) were located forward of the engine (a 5.75-gallon auxiliary

A DH 2 with the engine cowl panels removed, revealing the doped canvas bag that surrounded the fuel tank. (Alex Revell)

fuel tank was on the upper wing), surrounded by a doped canvas bag that collected fumes and fuel lost should the tanks be punctured and channelled them overboard via a drain pipe on the starboard undercarriage strut. Main tank fuel duration was two hours, and after tests showed that increasing fuel capacity to 26 gallons had a relatively unappreciable impact on performance, by August 1916 that capacity had been adopted as standard, which increased duration to 3.5 hours (including auxiliary tank).

Pilot engine management included a magneto switch, a fine adjustment wheel for fuel and an on/off 'blip switch' on top of the control column. There was no throttle – the Gnome Monosoupape was either off or running at full power – so the blip switch supplied a means of pilot engine control by 'blipping' or momentarily cutting off the magnetos that supplied current to the spark plugs. If there was no spark there was no combustion. The engine still rotated when blipped and fuel/air mixture was still drawn into the cylinders, so when the pilot released the blip switch after a short interval the spark returned and combustion began anew. The net effect was engine operation at less than full power.

Being an air-cooled rotary engine, the Gnome Monosoupape rotated with the propeller, which on early-production DH 2s was a fixed pitch, two-bladed wooden propeller made up of glued mahogany laminations by the Integral Propeller Company. In April 1916 tests showed the efficiency of a four-bladed propeller, and by that June all DH 2s in France were so equipped. Aircraft flown by training squadrons and the Middle East Brigade retained their two-bladed propellers, however. In either case, when 'three-pointed' on terra firma the pusher configuration brought the DH 2's rotating propeller blades into close proximity with the ground, where they were more susceptible to damage from stones and pebbles than were the blades of tractor-powered aeroplanes. To prevent this, pusher propeller tips were reinforced with doped fabric or brass sheaths.

Although slightly blurred, this photograph affords an excellent view of the DH 2 Monosoupape rotary engine spinning with the propeller. At such velocity, the damage wrought by a departing cylinder can be readily imagined. (Colin Owers via Aaron Weaver)

DH 2 COCKPIT

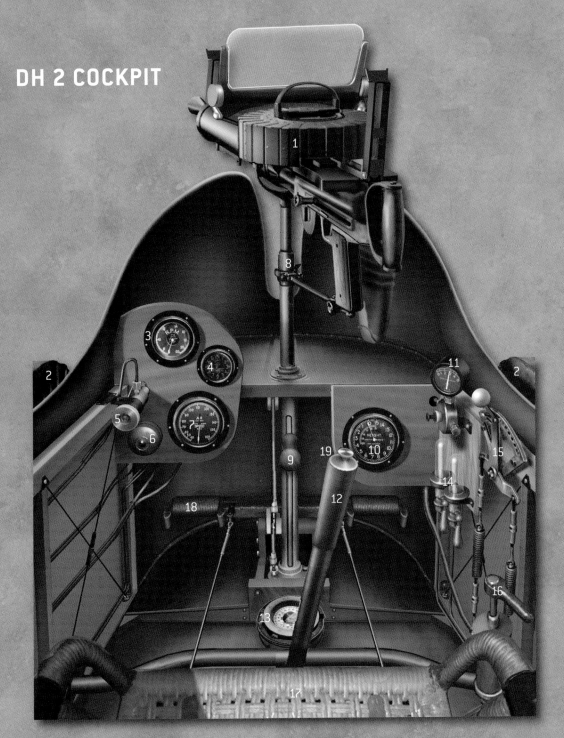

1. Lewis Mk 1 0.303in machine gun
2. Spare ammunition drums
3. Altimeter
4. Clock
5. Fuel fine adjustment wheel
6. Magneto switch
7. Airspeed indicator

8. Gun mounting bracket
9. Gun height adjustment lever
10. Tachometer
11. Air pressure gauge
12. Control column
13. Compass
14. Oil pulsator glasses

15. Elevator trim lever quadrant
16. Priming pump
17. Pilot's seat
18. Rudder bar
19. Ignition 'blip switch'

The DH 2's firepower consisted of a single forward-firing Lewis 0.303in machine gun with a rate of fire of approximately 550 rounds per minute. Early-production DH 2 gun mounts employed a flexible telescopic pillar – the so called 'Wobbly Mount' – that enabled pilots to swivel the gun freely as they flew. This created complex aiming solutions while airborne, so pilots preferred fixed mounts that allowed them to 'aim' the entire aeroplane. However, rendering the mounts stationary was prohibited officially, so pilots devised methods whereby the gun could be clipped stationary or unclipped to swivel freely. For example, future 57-victory ace Flt Sgt James McCudden of No. 29 Sqn wrote that when a 'Fokker passed above and in front of me I elevated my gun and fired a few shots at him from under his fuselage'.

The Lewis was fed ammunition via a top-mounted rotating drum that contained 47 rounds – later 'double drums' held 97, reducing the frequency of cumbersome in-flight drum replacement reloads – which were externally housed in wooden bins that bracketed the cockpit. Double drums were stored internally due to their larger sizes. A canvas deflector bag attached to the Lewis caught spent cartridge cases lest they foul the cockpit or blow back into the propeller to damage it. Later DH 2s are said to have had a chute that funnelled the cases into a faired collector bin under the nacelle nose.

The danger posed by spent cartridge cases is illustrated by McCudden's recollection that when what he identified as a 'Hun scout with a rotary engine and a very close gap' passed in front and above him, he raised his gun and fired at the German machine. However, his deflector bag was either missing or improperly seated, which allowed cartridge cases to impact and break the propeller and caused his immediate descent and forced dead-stick landing.

All of the above was housed within a stubby nacelle of cable-braced ash and spruce framework that supported a plywood floor and aluminium top and nose, with sides of stitched fabric. The pilot sat in a low-sided cockpit that was much more cramped than that of the Albatros D I or D II, restrained in his wicker seat by a wide lap belt.

Instrumentation included an altimeter, airspeed indicator, tachometer, bubble inclinometer, air pressure valve and gauge, oil pulsator glasses and a floor-mounted compass. A conventional control column and rudder bar provided pilot control about the axes, and elevator trim was provided by a sprung-lever quadrant on the starboard bell crank, to which the elevator control cables were connected. Due to the DH 2's pusher configuration, its pilots received no warming benefits from residual engine heat, and thus the cockpits were notoriously cold. Wrote McCudden:

> I have never experienced such cold as that which we went through on those de Havillands [DH 2s] at 12,000–13,000ft during December 1916. I remember that on one patrol I was so intensely cold and miserable that I did not trouble to look round at all to see whether any Huns were behind me or not. I was so utterly frozen. I cannot explain the intensity of the cold when high up in a 'pusher' aeroplane, but it can be readily remembered by those who have experienced it.

Aerodynamic lift was provided by four subtly tip-tapered wings of equal span that had different chords on either side of the boom attachments. The wings were rigged without stagger or sweepback, but employed approximately four degrees of dihedral, and all were identical. This in turn meant that they could be fitted in any port/starboard/upper/lower positions. The lower wings attached to the nacelle while the upper wings attached to a centre cabane section that connected to the nacelle via spruce struts just aft of the cockpit. The wings featured dual spar construction, with an internally braced spruce frame and three-ply ribs enveloped within a skin of doped fabric, and an aileron of similar construction was affixed to the outboard trailing edges of all four wings which enabled pilot control about the longitudinal axis.

The wings were rigged in such a way as to counter the torque produced by the propeller and spinning rotary engine, an effect of which was opposite roll about the longitudinal axis. This stabilised the machine when the engine was running, but when it was switched off or lost power from damage the DH 2 became unstable, which was a contributing factor in several accidents. Thus, squadrons and aircraft depots were instructed to rig the wings with equal washout, which ensured the wing roots stalled before the tips and gave pilots a measure of lateral control with the ailerons prior to the wings entering full stall.

In lieu of a fuselage the DH 2 had a common-for-pushers arrangement of twin upper and lower wire-braced and spruce strut-supported tubular steel booms that bracketed the propeller and extended back to the empennage, where the upper booms connected to the horizontal stabiliser and the lower booms attached in a V at the

Skeleton of the DH 2 prototype's nacelle, which was stripped of its fabric after capture by the Germans. The uncovered cable-braced framework reveals the pilot's proximity to the fuel tank and the scant room afforded between it and the Lewis machine gun. (Aaron Weaver)

rudder post. The empennage consisted of a steel tube framed and spruce ribbed horizontal stabiliser with a spruce framed vertical stabiliser above, all covered by doped fabric. The elevators and counter-balanced rudder were similarly constructed and controlled by the pilot via cables that led to the cockpit.

The empennage was supported by a spring-cushioned steel-shoed ash tailskid that was wired to the rudder control cables to afford a measure of ground steering, and the main undercarriage featured cable-braced ash V-struts to which a rubber cord sprung axle supported spoked wheels with 700mm × 75mm (25.5in × 2.95in) tyres. The normal wheel track was 5ft 9in, but No. 24 Sqn sought to improve ground handling and widened the track by fitting the wheels on the axle outside-in.

Performance specifications differ between the fuel tank installations, but generally the heavier tank did decrease performance somewhat. For example, what was once an 11-minute climb to 6,000ft became a 13-minute climb. However, much worse was the DH 2's chronic engine failure pandemic. Squadron record books and combat accounts are filled with reports of 'engine went dud', 'engine cutting out', 'engine going very badly' and 'engine missing and cutting out'. One pilot stated that his 'engine was missing and vibrating badly – landed, where several plugs and a tappet rod, which was bent, were changed, engine still running badly. On examination a rocker arm was found to be broken'. Another noted that his 'engine was missing and cutting out at intervals', while squadronmates stated 'engine cut out on two cylinders and started to knock' and 'engine ran well for first three-quarters of an hour then became rough and missed'.

If this were not bad enough, the DH 2 soon garnered a reputation for entering a spin that rumour stated was unrecoverable. After losing two pilots to spins and seeing fear creeping around the edges of his men, No. 24 Sqn commander Maj Lanoe Hawker took a DH 2 to 8,000ft and intentionally conducted a series of power-on and power-off spin tests to demonstrate that the aircraft was indeed recoverable. Afterwards, Hawker lectured the squadron on spin recovery procedure, and upon its successful employment the pilots' confidence in the nimble fighter grew.

Overall, the DH 2 was an initial success. Born from necessity to overcome the challenge of firing a machine gun through a spinning propeller arc, the fighter was sullied by rumour and hamstrung by engine problems. Yet it was flown into battle by the RFC, where it faced down the 'Fokker Scourge'. Thereafter the DH 2 enjoyed a summer of aerial superiority, until the pendulum of military might once again swung back toward the Germans.

DH 2 COLOURS AND MARKINGS

Production DH 2s featured light grey metal and wood components with clear doped fabric on the wings, empennage and nacelle sides. Blue/white/red roundels were applied outboard on the uppersurfaces of the upper wings and the undersurfaces of the lower wings, and the rudder was evenly divided into blue/white/red bands (from leading to trailing edge), with black serial numbers across the white and red bands. DH 2s of Nos. 24 and 29 Sqns arrived in France so finished.

In March 1916 squadron workshops began painting roundels on the fabric sides of the nacelle, the size, style and location of which varied between machines. That May the RFC required that all nacelles were to be painted grey, and in June all uppersurfaces were camouflaged with PC10, which generally had a chocolate brown to greenish khaki appearance that varied with age and length of ultraviolet light exposure. The grey nacelles were retained, although some machines did receive an overall PC10 finish. No. 32 Sqn machines arrived in France in this appearance.

In France No. 24 Sqn identified its three flights by colours, with red for 'A' Flight, white for 'B' Flight and blue for 'C' Flight. Each flight's DH 2s would have its representative colour applied to their fabric wheel covers. To identify individual machines within the flights they adopted the use of patterned bands on the outboard interplane struts – red and white for 'A' Flight, blue and white for 'B' Flight and black and white for 'C' Flight. Later, this identification was expanded to include large numbers on the wings and nacelle, the bottom of which was painted white and employed a 'sawtooth pattern' of grey or PC10.

No. 29 Sqn used numbers on the nacelle noses for identification, the colours of which were representative of each flight – 'A' Flight employed red numbers with white outlines or shadowing, 'B' Flight used white numbers with blue outlines or shadows and 'C' Flight used blue numbers outlined or shadowed in white.

No. 32 Sqn identified its flights with varying black and white concentric rings on the wheel covers. 'A' Flight used a thin white ring on a black background, 'B' Flight reversed this to have a thin black ring on a white background and 'C' Flight employed a central white disc on a black background. Later, the flights had their designated letter painted in white on the uppersurface of the port upper wing, with a white-painted number on the starboard wing. These were also featured in black on the nacelle undersurface.

No. 24 Sqn's Capt John Andrews casts a baleful glare before an early production DH 2. Note the machine gun is mounted further aft than those of later production machines, necessitating removal of the spade grips to afford more room for the pilot. (Alex Revell)

The business end of No. 32 Sqn DH 2 7851. The interchangeability of the wings is well evident in this view. Note the subtle aileron sag, fuselage ammunition bins outside the cockpit and the additional fairing surrounding the Lewis machine gun. (Colin Owers via Aaron Weaver)

DH 2 (26-gallon fuel tank variant)	
Dimensions	
Wingspan	28ft 3in
Chord (outside booms)	4ft 9in
Chord (inside booms)	3ft 11in
Dihedral	4.25 degrees
Length	25ft 2.5in
Height	9ft 7in
Armament	1 × Lewis Mk 1 0.303in machine gun
Weight (lb)	
Empty	943
Useful load	498
Loaded	1,441

Performance		
Engine	100hp Gnome Monosoupape	
	(20.8-gallon fuel tank)	(26-gallon fuel tank)
Maximum speed	93mph	93mph
Climb to 6,000ft	11 min	13 min
Climb to 8,000ft	17 min	19 min
Climb to 10,000ft	24 min 45 sec	29 min

ALBATROS D I AND D II

The Albatros D I and D II were born from the need to counter the numerous Nieuport and DH 2 fighters that had arrested the German monoplane fighter superiority and turned the tide of the 'Fokker Scourge' by late spring 1916. The key to the Albatros D I/II's success was its 160hp Mercedes F-1466 engine, commonly known as the Mercedes D III – a normally aspirated, direct-drive, water-cooled, carbureted, inline, overhead-cam, six-cylinder engine. Fuel and oil tanks were located immediately aft of the engine, all of which except the cylinders was cowled within detachable metal panels – there was no firewall.

Pilot engine management included a control column-mounted throttle, an auxiliary throttle control located port-forward in the cockpit and a spark-retarding lever on the port cockpit wall, along with an engine magneto switch key (which was removable and attached to a chain that in some photographs can be seen dangling outside of the cockpit) and starting magneto crank. Albatros engine starts did not employ ground personnel to 'swing' the propeller. Instead, the left engine magneto was switched on and the starting magneto hand-cranked from the cockpit, sending current

A close up of the Albatros D II cockpit. The control column supports the throttle (left) and machine gun triggers (centre), and the tachometer is just visible in the shadows under the forward cockpit coaming. The twin Maxims are shown to good effect, the ammunition bins of which form the 'front' of the cockpit. Note the flare cartridges at left and mirror above.

to the spark plugs that caused a continuous spark discharge within the cylinders that ignited the fuel/air mixture and started the engine.

Cooling was provided by port and starboard Windhoff fuselage-mounted radiators located just forward of the cockpit, with a triangular expansion tank fitted above the engine and slightly to port of the longitudinal axis. One early pre-production and all late-production D IIs replaced the Windhoff radiators with a Teeves und Braun radiator centrally mounted within the upper wing that was plumbed externally to carry coolant to and from the engine. This solid and reliable engine enabled the fully loaded D I to attain a maximum speed of 109mph in level flight and climb to 13,123ft in 30 minutes.

The Mercedes D III turned a fixed-pitch wooden propeller made of glued walnut and maple or walnut and ash laminations (import shortages of wood in 1916 also necessitated the use of teak, elm and pine), the hub of which was enclosed within a large aerodynamic spinner. Axial was a propeller manufacturer commonly used by Albatros, as were Garuda and Reschke, but regardless of manufacturer the 1916 *Idflieg Propellermerkbuch* (Propeller Notebook) stipulated that all propellers were to be kept clean, with the wood and metal parts greased strongly for moisture protection, especially in damp weather and after flights in fog or rain. Additionally, flight damage from raindrops or hail and erosion from sand and small pebbles picked up during taxiing degraded propeller performance and required that the damaged blade be 'sanded off and repainted on the aircraft – an easy task'.

The D I/II's firepower consisted of two fixed and forward firing Maxim lMG 08/15 7.92mm air-cooled machine guns, each synchronised to fire 500 rounds through the propeller arc at a rate of approximately 450 rounds per minute. This rate was an average dependent upon engine speed, and it varied greatly thanks to the differing propeller rpms used by the synchronisation gear to compensate for the variable frequency with which the blades passed before the gun muzzles. Despite the availability of Fokker's two-gun synchronisation gear, Albatros chose instead to devise and utilise an in-house two-gun synchronisation mechanism designed by *Werkmeister* Hedtke and modified by *Werkmeister* Semmler. Albatros apparently tested Fokker's mechanism in October 1916 but deemed the test unsuccessful and remained committed to the Hedtke system.

Triggers were centrally located on the control column near the throttle and situated so that the guns could be fired separately or simultaneously, and the gun breeches were pilot accessible for cocking and clearing jams. Hemp-belted cartridges were stored in magazines forward of the cockpit and fed to the guns via curved metal chutes, and after passing through the guns the empty belts descended separate chutes to collect in bins adjacent to the magazines – cartridge cases were ejected overboard. As with the engines, the guns were partially cowled within detachable metal panels.

The semi-monocoque wooden fuselage employed six longerons, to which was nailed a shellacked and varnished 2–3mm (0.1in) scarf-jointed, three-ply birch laminate skin. Within the leather-coamed open cockpit the pilot sat in a high-sided, padded bucket-type seat, adjustable fore and aft, with a four-point seatbelt and shoulder harness restraint. Instrumentation was sparse, even for the day, consisting of

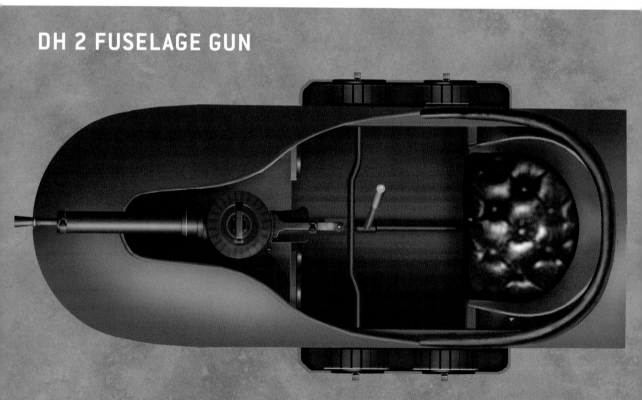

DH 2 FUSELAGE GUN

The DH 2 was armed with a single air-cooled Lewis Mk 1 machine gun, which was a gas-operated automatic weapon that fired 0.303in ammunition at a rate of approximately 550 rounds per minute. Bullets were stored in circular 47- or 97-cartridge magazines (or 'drums') that required changing by the pilot in combat – replacement 'drums' can be seen housed in external racks on either side of the cockpit. Although the normal and preferred Lewis mount was fixed, it could also be used in a flexible mode.

an engine tachometer, fuel valves and a floor-mounted compass. A conventional rudder bar and control column enabled pilot control about the axes, although there were neither brakes nor trim, and a small windscreen provided some protection from the slipstream. Overall, the D I/II cockpit was much more spacious and protective than that of the DH 2, and without an engine firewall the Albatros pilot enjoyed the warming benefits of radiant engine heat that the DH 2 pilot did not.

Lift was provided by two equal and constant chord, subtly tip-tapered wings of slightly unequal span that were affixed to the aeroplane with positive stagger, but without dihedral or sweepback. The upper wing was a one-piece structure that attached to the fuselage via inverted V-struts (similar to those employed on the Albatros C-types) that were slotted to permit fore or aft adjustment of stagger.

Here, the D I and D II differed markedly, with the former's inverted V-struts giving way to the D II's outwardly splayed N-struts and its wing gap reduced by lowering the upper wing by 9.8in. Both upper and lower wings featured dual spar construction, with internally wire-braced plywood ribs enclosed within a skin of doped fabric (which pulled against the approximately 1mm (0.3in)-diameter wire trailing edge to create the classic scalloped appearance). They were braced externally with wire rigging and streamlined steel struts, and steel-tubed, fabric-covered ailerons located on the port

ALBATROS D II FUSELAGE GUNS

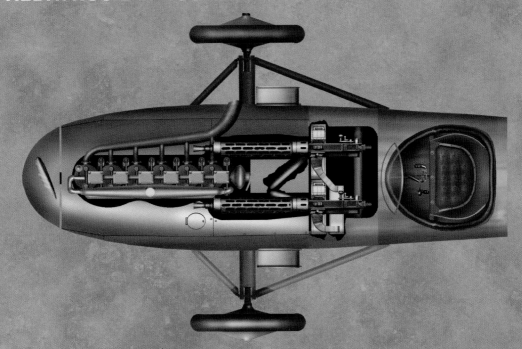

The Albatros D II (like the D I) was armed with two fixed air-cooled Maxim IMG 08/15 machine guns that were synchronised to fire through the spinning propeller arc, each gun being belt-fed 500 7.92mm cartridges. Rate-of-fire was set at approximately 450 rounds per minute per gun, although engine RPM altered this rate significantly to compensate for the variable frequency with which the propeller blades passed before the gun muzzles.

The sharp end of Oblt Rudolf Berthold's Albatros D II D.1717/16 illustrates the closely cowled Mercedes D III engine and nestled machine guns. The gap between the spinner and the front cowls — secured in part by spring fasteners — is well evident, as is Berthold's large, non-standard windscreen. (Greg VanWyngarden)

and starboard outboard upper wing trailing edges provided lateral control about the aeroplane's longitudinal axis.

The wood-framed empennage featured a ply-covered vertical stabiliser and two fabric-covered horizontal stabilisers, all of which employed curved leading edges and low aspect ratios. The steel-tube framed counter-balanced rudder and one-piece elevator were covered with doped fabric and operated via cables that fed through the fuselage and into the cockpit, and a one-piece steel-shoed ash tailskid supported the empennage, which was bungeed for a measure of shock absorption. Similarly, the main landing gear employed bungeed shock absorption that also served to connect the steel-tube V-struts to the wheel axle, and a steel restraining cable was used to limit axle travel and prevented gear collapse in the event of bungee failure.

Performance specifications of the various D I and D II builds were fairly consistent between the types. Official D II specifications list it as 46lb lighter than the D I – ostensibly this figure relates to late-production D IIs that had one instead of two radiators – and thus the D II had a slightly better rate of climb, although overall both models were sleek and rugged war machines. More powerful than their DH 2

These *Jasta* 6 machines afford an excellent view of the visual differences between the Albatros D II (centre, Vzfw Carl Holler's D.454/16) and D I (right). Note the D II's reduced wing gap afforded pilots greater visibility above and forward. (Greg VanWyngarden)

32

ALBATROS D II COCKPIT

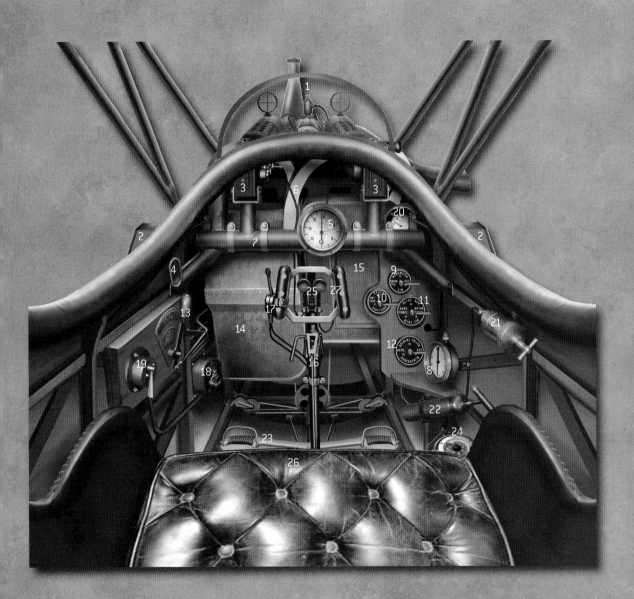

1. Windscreen
2. Engine coolant radiators
3. 7.92mm IMG 08/15 machine guns
4. Auxiliary throttle handle
5. Tachometer
6. Spent ammunition belt chute
7. Mounting bar for guns and instruments
8. Fuel quantity gauge
9. Fuel pressure gauge valve

10. Fuel tank pressure valve
11. Air pump selector valve
12. Fuel tank selector valve
13. Spark control handle
14. Spent ammunition belt can
15. Ammunition belt containers in front of spent ammunition belt can
16. Control column
17. Throttle handle
18. Starting magneto

19. Magneto switch key
20. Fuel pressure gauge
21. Water pump greaser
22. Hand-operated air pump
23. Rudder control bar
24. Magnetic compass
25. Machine gun fire buttons
26. Adjustable leather-padded aluminium seat
27. Control column grip

adversaries, they had better firepower, more reliable engines and cockpits that afforded considerably better protection for the pilot from the elements. With these machines the *Fliegertruppe* and *Luftstreitkräfte* took control of the Western Front skies in autumn 1916. They duly passed that baton on to their successor the Albatros D III, which, although hamstrung initially with significant structural teething troubles, continued to hold sway over the RFC well into the summer of 1917.

ALBATROS D I/II COLOURS AND MARKINGS

Although produced by three different manufacturing companies (Albatros Flugzeugwerke at Johannisthal, Ostdeutsche Albatros Werke (OAW) at Schneidmühl and Luftverkehrsgesellschaft (LVG), also at Johannisthal) that employed camouflage variations, most production Albatros D I/IIs boasted a high-gloss shellacked and varnished birch fuselage that has been described as appearing 'warm straw yellow'. The spinner, engine cowling panels, fittings, access hatches, vents and cabane/interplane/undercarriage struts were either light grey, pale greenish grey or greenish beige.

The fuselage employed an ovoid cross-section up to the leading edge of the wings, where it became vertically slab-sided back to the tip of the tail, although throughout its length its spine and belly retained their ovoid curves. The intersection of the curved belly and slab-sided fuselage at the lower wing leading and trailing edge connection points created drag-producing protuberances that required the installation of either wood or metal aerodynamic fairings.

The wheel covers and undersurfaces of the wings, ailerons, horizontal stabilisers and elevator were painted light blue, but the uppersurfaces and national markings varied between the individual manufacturers. Albatros Flugzeugwerke's Johannisthal-built D Is 422 to 471/16 and D IIs 472 to 521/16 and 1700 to 1799/16 featured wing uppersurfaces that employed a two-tone camouflage of Venetian red and olive green or three-tone camouflage of Venetian red, olive green and pale green. The pattern of camouflage colours and their port or starboard directional slant varied between machines. The fabric-covered rudder could be either clear doped linen or often one of the various camouflage colours. Again, this varied between machines.

National markings consisted of a black *Eisernkreuz* on a square white crossfield at eight points. There was one on each upper and lower wingtip (although some lower wing crosses were applied directly to the blue undersurfaces without a white crossfield or border), one on each side of the fuselage well aft near the horizontal stabiliser and one on each side of the tail, overlapping the hinge line of the vertical stabiliser and the rudder. A black serial number such as 'D.481/16' was hand-painted on either side of the vertical stabiliser, and although similar, no two numbers were alike. The 'D' in the serial represented the aircraft designation (single-engined single-seat biplane with armament), '481' denoted that it was the tenth machine of the first production batch (D.472 to 521/16) and '/16' was the last two digits of the year it was ordered.

Manufacturer and *Idflieg* placards were located on either side of the nose and on the leading edge of the lower wings, just outboard of the interplane struts. Finally, an Albatros company logo (a helmeted bird with wings spread in flight) adorned either side of the rudder, this symbol being applied so that both port and starboard birds faced (i.e. 'flew towards') the spinner.

Additionally, some Albatrosses had their fuselages camouflaged in bands of olive green and rust brown, with the fuselage bottom painted pale blue and a subtly feathered demarcation between the upper and lower surfaces. Furthermore, other Albatros fuselages may have been stained reddish-brown and varnished, based on an *Idflieg* document stating 'experiments by the Albatros firm have proved that colouring the fuselage (plywood parts) is possible without an appreciable increase in the all up weight (50 grams)'.

Albatros D II (OAW) D.933/16's arboreous demise provides a good view of the rough camouflage demarcations that are characteristic of OAW-built machines. Note the full-dark elevator and high-gloss finish of the wooden fuselage. (Greg VanWyngarden)

Ostdeutsche Albatros Werke D IIs 890 to 939/16 were finished similarly to their Johannisthal brethren. This meant warm straw yellow fuselages, grey or greyish beige metal fittings and the wings and horizontal stabilisers/elevator painted in what has been described as 'patches of burnt sienna and light and dark green blending into one another'. Photographs, however, reveal that this 'blending' was often very coarse and rough, with 'undersurfaces a very pale blue'. Other OAW machines had their fuselages camouflaged in the same manner, and colours, as the wings, including the coarse blending, with their bellies light blue from nose cowl to tailskid. The engine panels remained a shade of grey.

Eisernkreuz national markings were located at the usual eight points, all of which bore a 5cm (1.9in) white border instead of a square crossfield, and the fuselage crosses were located further forward than those on the Johannisthal machines. Serial numbers were allocated to the wheel covers rather than the vertical stabiliser, and the fuselage manufacturer and *Idflieg* placards were located just below the cockpit.

Luftverkehrsgesellschaft D IIs 1024 to 1098/16 shared the Albatros Flugzeugwerke machine's warm straw yellow fuselage colour too, with the standard greyish metal fittings. Wing root fairings were often left unpainted in wood finish. Wings, horizontal stabiliser and elevator camouflage was distinctive in its appearance, with light and dark bands of burnt sienna, dark green and light Brunswick green that were diagonally mirrored on either side of the centreline. Wing undersurfaces have been described as 'pale greenish-blue' or 'duck egg green' and the rudder was normally one of the uppersurface camouflage colours.

National markings were in the usual eight-point positions, initially on white crossfields, but these were later replaced by white-bordered crosses, although some machines displayed both types. Serial numbers were not seen on the vertical stabilisers.

35

As illustrated on this Albatros D III, the vast majority of Johannisthal-built D-types had their rudder logos affixed so that the Albatros faced or 'flew toward' the spinner – i.e., faced left on the port side and right on the starboard, although there were occasional exceptions. (Albatros logo Michael Backus)

The D I/II's autumnal arrival in 1916 coincided with the formation of the *Jagdstaffeln*, but generally the aircraft were not overpainted in garish colours and markings to the degree the Germans employed by the following spring. However, various *Staffeln* did use unit markings, such as *Jasta* 23's swastika, while others based their markings on a 'theme', such as *Jasta* 2's abbreviated pilot names (although Ltn Manfred von Richthofen and Oblt Stefan Kirmaier preferred vertical stripes, and *Staffelführer* Hptm Oswald Boelcke used nothing at all). *Jasta* 5 used individual letters and geometric symbols were a feature of *Kampfstaffel* 11, *Kampfgeschwader* 2 machines.

Individual markings were not unknown either, such as *Jasta* 22 Josef Jacobs' *'Kobe'* or Prince Friedrich Karl's skull and crossbones, inspired by his prior service with the 'Death's Head Hussars' *1.Leib-Husaren-Regiment Nr. 1*. Entire fuselage overpainting was also seen on occasion too, with several *Jasta* 2 machines boasting green or brown (including that flown by the Prince) schemes, although again this practice was neither as common nor ostentatiously employed as would be seen during the following year.

The business end of an Albatros D II. Displaying the characteristic LVG-style camouflage, this machine displays prominent Windhoff radiators, an Axial propeller and an anemometer airspeed indicator on the lower starboard wing.

Albatros D I D.391/16 of *Jasta* 2's Ltn Karl Büttner after his downing and capture on 16 November 1916. Although emblazoned with RFC markings, the machine retained its overpainted fuselage aft of the nose cowl, as seen on many *Jasta* 2 machines. (Aaron Weaver)

Albatros	D I	D II
Engine	160hp Mercedes D III	160hp Mercedes D III
Wingspan (upper)	27ft 11in	27ft 11in
Wingspan (lower)	26ft 3in	26ft 3in
Chord (upper wing)	5ft 3in	5ft 3in
Chord (lower wing)	5ft 3in	5ft 3in
Dihedral	none	none
Length	24ft 3in	24ft 3in
Height	9ft 8in	8ft 8in
Armament	2 × 7.92mm IMG 08/15s	2 × 7.92mm IMG 08/15s
Weight (lb)		
Empty	1,530	1,484
Useful load	502	496
Loaded	2,032	1,980
Maximum speed (mph)	109	109
Climb to 1,000m (3,281ft)	4 min	4 min
Climb to 2,000m (6,562ft)	10 min	10 min
Climb to 3,000m (9,843ft)	19 min	19 min
Climb to 4,000m (13,123ft)	30 min	30 min

THE STRATEGIC SITUATION

Immediately after World War I broke out in August 1914, the French army, led by Gen Joseph Joffre, clung to a pre-war plan predicated on the expectation that any German attack would come from the east via the Ardennes. So minded, it was caught off-guard when German forces greatly in excess of those estimated pushed instead into northern France via neutral Belgium. Joffre had known of the German presence in Belgium but steadfastly believed that it was actually a feint by the enemy to pull the main French forces away from their positions in the Ardennes, and thus he would not redeploy his troops. Instead, he ordered the Belgian army to hold until French forces could be spared.

On the British side, Field Marshal Sir John French had proposed that instead of adhering to the original plan to support the French army directly, British forces could be deployed north to Antwerp to aid the Belgians, who faced not a feint but the main German thrust – he was overruled. Thus, the German army was able to rout the ill-prepared Belgian army, penetrate France north of her main forces and then push south toward Paris. Thereafter, British and French forces engaged in a fighting retreat, peppered with offensive thrusts that endured shocking casualties and failed to halt the advance. Soon, the Germans were within 30 miles of Paris.

At this point Sir John French considered the French army beaten, and he expressed a desire to withdraw all British troops. Such action would have been considered a violation of pre-war treaties, however, and he was persuaded to support Gen Joffre's embattled forces.

The battered Allies then launched a coordinated series of counter-attacks during the Battle of the Marne between 5 and 10 September 1914, these finally halting the

German advance which, by then, had been hampered by combat losses and stretched communications and supply lines. With its left flank and rear now vulnerable, the German army conducted a general withdrawal to the Aisne River, where troops dug in and established defensive positions. When these could not be breached the opposing forces attempted to outflank each other to the north, and in so doing built elaborate systems of defensive trenches as they moved further and further away from Paris until they were finally stopped by the North Sea.

From then on the war's first weeks of offensive mobility gave way to the defensive static trench warfare of 'No Man's Land', and by 1915 the conflict that was supposed to have been over by Christmas was deadlocked, with no end in sight. Winston Churchill wrote that the outcome of World War I 'was decided in the first 20 days of fighting, and all that happened afterwards consisted of battles which, however formidable and devastating, were but desperate and vain appeals against the decision of fate'.

Indeed, the first full year of the war saw little change along these trenches except failed offensives and a mounting death toll. By the end of 1915 1,292,000 French soldiers, 612,000 German soldiers and 279,000 British soldiers had been killed or wounded (these figures are approximate as casualty figures vary). Any territorial advancement bought by these casualties came in the form of mere yards. On Christmas Day 1915, German Gen Erich von Falkenhayn sent a letter to Kaiser Wilhelm II stating that for France, 'The strain [of the war] has reached the breaking point – though it is certainly borne with the most remarkable devotion. If we succeed in opening the eyes of her people to the fact that in a military sense they have nothing more to hope for, that breaking point would be reached and England's best sword knocked out of her hand.'

Thus, in order to 'bleed France white', von Falkenhayn formulated and executed an offensive against the French city of Verdun – an important fortress that he knew the French would defend at all cost. The German plan was not so much to capture Verdun but rather provoke the French into a series of counter-attacks, during which they would be annihilated. Although final figures differ, the French indeed suffered appalling casualties as they held Verdun during the 1916 siege, with some 542,000 men killed or wounded. Yet they were not the only ones being bled white, for German losses were some 434,000 killed or wounded. The mutual exsanguinations ultimately led to von Falkenhayn being relieved of this command and replaced by Gen Paul von Hindenburg, although the latter's deputy, Gen Erich Ludendorff, exercised the real power, serving as the de facto general chief of staff.

During these series of stygian ground campaigns air power played an important yet initially less lethal role, namely via reconnaissance – crucial for armies to formulate strategy. While tethered observation balloons performed this service along both sides of the front, aerial observation via photo-reconnaissance aeroplanes became increasingly important as it provided strategists with valuable real-time views of enemy forces that would not have been attainable otherwise.

Initially, these observation aeroplanes – two-seater machines with a pilot and dedicated observer – flew about unmolested, save for anti-aircraft fire, but upon the continued furtherance of reconnaissance sorties the opposing machines encountered each other with increasing frequency. Inevitably, crews started taking rifles aloft to exchange potshots with their enemy counterparts. Obviously, the value of attaining an aerial reconnaissance advantage over one's enemy while denying him same was so clear that eventually both sides sought to prosecute the development of quick, single-seat 'scouts' for the purpose of two-seater reconnaissance interdiction and destruction.

These single-seaters were initially hamstrung by the problem of synchronising a forward-firing machine gun to shoot through a spinning propeller arc – it could not be done. French and German efforts to synchronise machine gun fire had commenced in 1910, although they enjoyed little to no military support and were hampered by 'hang fires' that disrupted the required steady gunfire cadence. By 1914 French aeroplane manufacturer Morane-Saulnier had developed a synchroniser gear, but ground gunnery tests subsequently revealed that some bullets still struck the propeller due to 'hang fires' and the irregular rate of fire of open-bolt light machine guns then in use.

While sorting out these teething troubles, Raymond Saulnier devised a backup solution of also installing steel wedges to the propeller that deflected the bullets that would have otherwise shattered the wooden blades. These wedges underwent several successful tests until one apparently detached in flight, causing a significant imbalance that required shutting off the engine and initiating a forced landing.

Further tests were delayed due to aeroplane repairs and the redesigning of the propeller to better mount the deflector wedges, but in early 1915 French pilot Sgt Roland Garros, who as a civilian had conducted some of the pre-war test flights in 1914, proposed trying the device again in action. He duly used his modified aeroplane to shoot down three German machines in two weeks. Unfortunately, on 18 April engine failure led to Garros' forced landing and the capture of the device, which was then delivered to Doberitz for evaluation by *Idflieg*, with the expectation of improving it for use on German machines.

One man contacted to do this was Dutchman Anthony Fokker, for whom the timing was perfect. His Fokker Aeroplanbau had already been working for months on a means by which a fixed machine gun could be fired through a propeller arc via an interrupter gear. The Fokker system, which is believed to have been based on a 1913 patent held by Franz Schneider, a Swiss employed by the German firm Luftverkehrsgesellschaft (LVG), prevented the weapon from firing whenever a propeller blade passed before the muzzle. Demonstrating this device at Doberitz a month after the capture of Saulnier's synchroniser gear, Fokker was awarded a production contract to produce interrupter gear-equipped aeroplanes. As German *Fliegertruppe* Commander Gen Ernst von Hoeppner subsequently wrote in post-war memoirs:

> The true *Kampfflugzeug* [combat aeroplane] originated first with the utilisation of Fokker's invention, which made it possible to fire through the propeller arc. The fixed machine gun was now operated by the pilot himself. The omission of the observer produced in this new E-type aeroplane extraordinary speed, manoeuvrability and climbing ability.

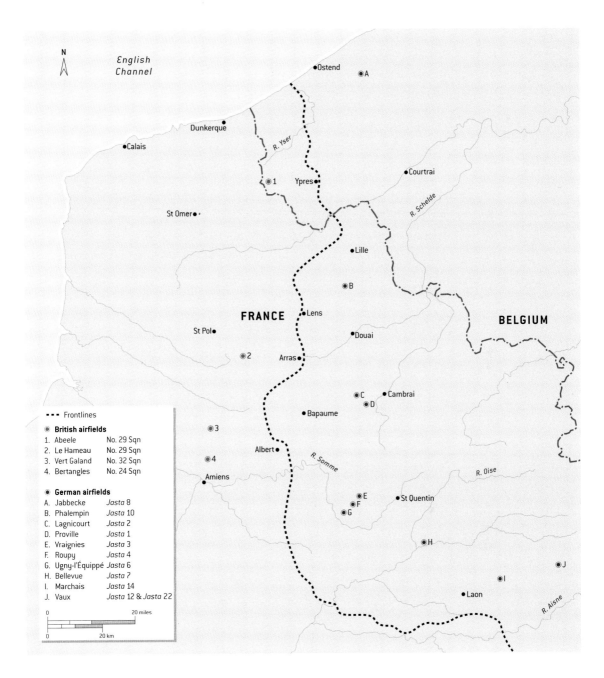

N

English
Channel

●Ostend ◉A

●Calais

Dunkerque

R. Yser

◉1 Ypres●

St Omer●

●Courtrai

R. Schelde

●Lille

◉B

FRANCE ●Lens

St Pol●

●Douai

◉2 Arras●

BELGIUM

◉C ●Cambrai
◉D

●Bapaume

◉3

Albert●

R. Somme

R. Oise

◉4

Amiens●

◉E ●St Quentin
◉F
◉G

◉H

◉J

◉I

●Laon

R. Aisne

- - - Frontlines

◉ **British airfields**
1. Abeele   No. 29 Sqn
2. Le Hameau   No. 29 Sqn
3. Vert Galand No. 32 Sqn
4. Bertangles   No. 24 Sqn

◉ **German airfields**
A. Jabbecke   *Jasta* 8
B. Phalempin   *Jasta* 10
C. Lagnicourt   *Jasta* 2
D. Proville   *Jasta* 1
E. Vraignies   *Jasta* 3
F. Roupy   *Jasta* 4
G. Ugny-l'Équippé *Jasta* 6
H. Bellevue   *Jasta* 7
I. Marchais   *Jasta* 14
J. Vaux   *Jasta 12 & Jasta 22*

0   20 miles

0   20 km

This new E-type was the Fokker E I, a mid-wing monoplane powered by an air-cooled 80hp rotary engine. By mid 1915 German pilots were using this new weapon to attack Allied reconnaissance aeroplanes, ushering in a desperate period for the Allies during which Germany held air superiority. Initially, the Allies had no effective machine with which to counter this threat, and necessarily changed their tactics to state that 'a machine proceeding on reconnaissance must be escorted by at least three other fighting machines, and a reconnaissance should not be continued if any machines become detached'. Four aeroplanes were now required to do the work of one.

Meanwhile, as the horror of Verdun trudged through 1916, the French had urged a British offensive to lessen France's military burden. Toward that end the British army initiated the Battle of the Somme on 1 July. However, by this time the 'Fokker Scourge' had been effectively countered by the arrival of Allied single-seater fighters, namely the French Nieuports. As the British and German armies slogged through yet another bloodbath – British casualties on the first day of the Battle of the Somme alone were some 19,000 killed and 41,000 wounded – the Geoffrey de Havilland designed FE 2 and DH 2 pushers were dominating the skies.

Since arriving in France the previous February DH 2s had routinely clashed with the German monoplanes, and by the end of May the pusher units enjoyed complete air superiority, which they maintained throughout the summer. The introduction of German single-seat and single-gun biplane fighters failed to alter the tide as the Somme battles flared on and off in a series of small attacks and counter-attacks, and on 15 September the British launched an offensive known as the Battle of Flers-Courcelette, using tanks for the first time.

Unfortunately, this offensive coincided with a restructuring of the German air force and the arrival of its first inline-engined twin-gun fighters, the Albatros D I and D II. During the autumn of 1916 the DH 2 engaged these machines in a valiant struggle, and although a number of victories were claimed, they could not stop them from swinging the pendulum of air superiority back in Germany's favour. Achieving the latter would not be easy, however, and by year end both sides would lose crucial and well-loved flight leaders in epic clashes – those between No. 24 Sqn and *Jagdstaffel* 2 in particular would become the stuff of legend. Fledglings forced to cut their teeth on mortal experience during this period would rise as leaders anew to shoulder the aerial burdens of the desperate months ahead.

THE COMBATANTS

ROYAL FLYING CORPS

In 1915 the German deployment of the Fokker Eindecker, with its synchronised machine gun, caused such casualty and concern amongst the RFC's bombing and reconnaissance two-seaters that by year end squadrons equipped with these types had been notified that 'until the Royal Flying Corps is in possession of a machine as good as or better than the German Fokker it seems necessary that a change in tactics employed becomes necessary [sic]. It is hoped very shortly to obtain a machine which will successfully engage the Fokkers at present in use by the Germans'.

The DH 2's arrival coincided with the implementation of squadrons dedicated to the use of single-seat fighters, and because most prior pilot experience had been gleaned via much more stable two-seater tractor machines such as the BE 2, training was necessary for aviators to make the adjustment to a single-seat rotary pusher. Even pilots with pusher experience had to become accustomed to the DH 2, as No. 24 Sqn 2Lt John Andrews recalled in later years:

One had to get accustomed to that very marked engine torque, which rocked the aeroplane, and tended to turn it instead of the airscrew. In those days, the rotary engines had no throttle – you controlled the engine by switching it on and switching it off. There was a switch on the joystick, a 'blip' switch, and if you wanted to cut the engine out, you couldn't throttle it back – you switched it right off, and when you wanted power, you took your thumb off the switch and the engine came on again. It was either all or nothing, and whenever you changed from one to the other you affected the lateral trim of the aircraft by the engine power suddenly coming on or cutting out, which was different, of course, from the stationary engine like the BE 2 or the Maurice Farman – they had throttles.

JOHN OLIVER ANDREWS

The son of a brewer, John Oliver Andrews was born on 20 July 1896 in Waterloo, Lancashire. He graduated from Manchester High School in 1912, and two years later joined The Royal Scots as a 2nd Lieutenant. Shortly thereafter Andrews was seconded to the RFC for training as an observer, and in that capacity he served with No. 5 Sqn in 1915. Realising the war was going to be much longer than anticipated, Andrews trained to be a pilot and received his Royal Aero Club certificate in October 1915. He then joined No. 24 Sqn, which was forming in England. With that unit he trained to fly DH 2s, about which he recalled:

> The DH 2 was quite a tricky little aeroplane, very different from the tractors [engine and propeller in front of the pilot] in which I'd done most of my flying. I had flown pusher types, such as the Farman and the Vickers, but the DH 2 had a much smaller wingspan, was more heavily loaded and the torque of the comparatively large engine in a small frame was somewhat unusual in an aircraft of that period.

In February 1916 No. 24 Sqn travelled to France, and by that autumn Andrews had been credited with seven victories, including *Jasta* 2 *Staffelführer* and Boelcke successor Oblt Stefan Kirmaier. The following day he was involved in the fight with *Jasta* 2 that saw No. 24 Sqn's CO and RFC luminary Maj Lanoe Hawker shot down and killed by the rising *Jasta* 2 star Manfred von Richthofen. Andrews had been disabled early in the fight, recalling:

> I was shot to pieces from behind straightaway – tanks, engine and the rest – and all I could do was turn in the direction of the lines in the hope that I could run a straight glide. I'd got no engine to manoeuvre and no height to spare, and I hoped that I could just scrape over the trenches, which is what I did. The whole machine was riddled like a colander when I got it on the ground. I managed to land, though, and the right way up.

Afterwards, Andrews flew Sopwith Pups as a No. 66 Sqn flight commander and later commanded the RAF's

No. 209 Sqn on the Western Front. After the war the veteran ace led No. 221 Sqn fighting the Bolsheviks in south Russia, served as squadron leader with the Aeronautical Committee of Guarantee in Germany, attended Cambridge and London universities and qualified as a German Interpreter, First Class, attended the Imperial Defence College and became a Senior Air Staff Officer in the Far East.

During World War II Andrews was made Director of Armament Development at the Air Ministry, and he was very much involved with the structure and organisation of Home Defence, which played a crucial role during the Battle of Britain in 1940. 'It was very well organised – had it not been, I shouldn't be here today', quipped Andrews in a post-war interview.

John Andrews retired from the RAF with the rank of air vice-marshal in 1945 and subsequently passed away on 29 May 1989, aged 92.

OSWALD BOELCKE

The fourth child of a high school professor, Oswald Boelcke was born on 19 May 1891 in the Halle suburb of Giebichenstein, in Saxony. The family subsequently moved to Dessau, where Boelcke graduated from the Friedrichs Gymnasium in 1911. He then joined the Prussian Cadet Corps Telegrapher's Battalion, with whom he served until an interest in aviation led to Boelcke transferring to the *Fliegertruppe* and becoming a pilot in 1914.

When World War I began that August Boelcke was assigned to *Flieger Abteilung* (Flying Unit/Section) 13, flying two-seaters with his brother Wilhelm as observer. By February 1915 he had received the Iron Cross First and Second classes. Flying an LVG C I with *Feldflieger Abteilung* (Field Aviation Unit) 62, Boelcke and his new observer scored a victory over a Morane Parasol on 4 July 1915, and thereafter he was driven by an interest in aerial combat which led to him flying single-seat Fokker Eindeckers. Via this new form of warfare he shot down several more Allied aeroplanes in the autumn of 1915 during the infamous 'Fokker Scourge', and for this outstanding achievement Boelcke was awarded the *Orden Pour le Mérite* on 12 January 1916.

Upon the death of *FFA* 62 comrade and rival Max Immelmann that June, Boelcke was grounded and given the choice of a desk job or an 'inspection tour' of the Balkans, lest he too be killed and further damage national morale. He chose the latter option. Prior to his departure Boelcke visited with the *Feldflugchef* (Aviation Chief of Staff) and discussed his principles for aerial combat (the famous 'Dicta Boelcke'), emphasised the need for permanent single-seater units and suggested that pilots should adhere to strict formation flying.

During the inspection tour the British Somme offensive commenced, and in August Boelcke was ordered back to the Western Front to form and lead a squadron (which became *Jagdstaffel* 2 (Hunting Squadron 2)) of single-seat fighters in the restructuring German air force. There, he trained a group of hand-picked neophytes – including Manfred von Richthofen, Erwin Böhme and Max Müller, all future *Orden Pour le Mérite* winners – to become fighter pilots. His lessons centred on the articles

of his 'Dicta', particularly those of securing advantage before attacking, firing only at close range and carrying through an attack once begun. Under Boelcke's tutelage *Jasta* 2 quickly became the paramount *Jagdstaffel*, and during that autumn it helped Germany wrest back control of the skies.

By 28 October 1916 Boelcke's victory tally had reached 40, but during his sixth sortie that day a mid-air collision with Böhme led to his fatal crash. The impact had been minor, Böhme writing that 'it was only a light touch, but at such breakneck speeds that also meant a strong impact'. The damage to his upper left wing progressively spread and Boelcke was unable to maintain sufficient control to prevent his fighter from crashing. His body was recovered, and after a funeral service at Cambrai Cathedral that was 'like that of a reigning prince' Boelcke was transported back to his home town of Dessau for burial. He was 25.

You had to be very careful to take no risks near the ground until you got a proper feel for the machine. There was a particular problem with spinning. Any aircraft that stalled easily and was laterally unstable on account of the engine torque tended to get into a spin. With the DH 2, things happened very suddenly because of this torque, and unless you spotted it and corrected it at once, you could get into a spin or stall the engine.

It was a very handy little aeroplane when the engine was functioning properly, and it had quite a lot of horses for the size of the aircraft, so it gave quite good performance.

The first DH 2s arrived at No. 24 Sqn – the first RFC unit dedicated to employing single-seat fighters – in January 1916 while still working up at Hendon in northwest London. Unfortunately, their Gnome Monosoupape engines were so unreliable that it was necessary to husband the allowable training time to less than two hours to ensure that the machines could be flown to France with a reasonable expectation of crossing the English Channel without engine failure! This No. 24 Sqn did on 7 February, after which the pilots conducted practice flights and patrols behind the lines.

By the 13th two pilots had perished in accidents caused by spins, and although No. 24 Sqn commander Maj Lanoe Hawker's spin recovery demonstrations instilled pilot confidence in their stick-and-rudder abilities with their new pusher aeroplanes, the rampant engine troubles continued. Rings, magnetos, tappets and rocker arms all failed regularly, and the Monosoupape was known to throw a cylinder from the crankcase – coined 'cylindritis' – which had disastrous results if the departing cylinder struck and detached a tail boom supporting the empennage. Unfortunately, although engine problems lessened as time passed, they were always common with DH 2 operations. This was as much of a hazard for pilots as combat.

FLIEGERTRUPPE

Such concerns were far less pressing for the Germans. The new Mercedes engines in their Albatros D I/IIs were extremely reliable and of an inline configuration with which pilots were familiar and had plenty of operating experience.

Unlike their British counterparts who required the private acquisition of a pilot certificate before being accepted into the RFC, German aviators usually requested transfer into the *Fliegertruppe*, often as observers, before receiving flight training to become two-seater pilots – sometimes by unofficial means, such as with World War I's top-scoring ace Manfred von Richthofen, who as an observer was taught to fly by his pilot after and in between their scheduled sorties.

Many of these pilots cut their teeth flying two-seaters (Albatros C III, LFG Roland C II, LVG C II, Rumpler C I etc.) powered by the same 160hp Mercedes D III engine fitted in the Albatros D I/II, so for aviators transitioning to Albatros single-seaters the conversion 'row-to-hoe' was much easier than for pilots transitioning to a rotary pusher.

Even so, pilots of the new *Jasta* 2 faced a similar problem to their counterparts in No. 24 Sqn in respect to limited training and conversion time, but for an entirely

different reason – lack of aeroplanes. Upon his recall to the Western Front Hptm Oswald Boelcke had assembled his new *Staffel* at Bertincourt aerodrome, but during the first two weeks of its existence only a solitary Albatros D I from neighbouring *Jasta* 1 had arrived to join a rag-tag collection comprising in toto a Fokker D I, Fokker D III and one 'refurbished' Halberstadt D-type!

Boelcke flew solo patrols in the Fokker D III while the rest of the *Staffel* shared the remaining three aeroplanes, so their time in the air was limited, especially when it came to flying the lone Albatros D I. Finally, on 16 September, five Albatros D Is and a single Albatros D II for Boelcke (equipped with a Teeves und Braun wing radiator rather than the D I's fuselage-mounted Windhoffs) arrived for *Jasta* 2. This still left the *Staffel* short of machines, but signified an end to the pilots' drought, and just in time, since Boelcke wrote 'my pilots are all passionately keen and very competent, but I must first train them to steady teamwork – they are at present rather like young puppies in their zeal to achieve something'.

No. 32 Sqn DH 2 7862 fitted with Le Prieur rocket tubes, although the rockets themselves are absent. The outboard interplane struts and adjacent uppersurfaces of the lower wings have been protected against rocket exhaust. (Aaron Weaver)

Albatros D I D.435/16 featured a camouflaged fuselage with pale blue undersurfaces. Its Axial propeller displays the early 'dagger' style logo. (Aaron Weaver)

47

Achieve something they did forthwith, flying with Boelcke in their new machines on 17 September and finding trouble immediately. None had more than a few hours in an Albatros D-type, if any at all, yet they had studiously absorbed their leader's tactics lectures and were able to apply them in battle without the encumbrance of transitioning to a single-seat rotary pusher, as did the RFC DH 2 pilots.

LUFTSTREITKRÄFTE

On 8 October 1916 Gen Ernst von Hoeppner was promoted to *Kommandierenden General der Luftstreitkräfte* (*Kogenluft*), which meant that he was responsible to the Chief of the General Staff of the Armies in the Field for the use of all German air forces at the front, and for training and unit formation at home. This included all flying formations in the field, army airships at the front, the Meteorological service, the *Flugabwehrkanonen* (*Flak*) and the organisation of the aerial defence of Germany.

Much of the reorganisation that followed von Hoeppner's appointment was born from lessons learned at Verdun and the Somme, where the importance of single-seater aeroplanes in the destruction of enemy aircraft had been amply demonstrated. Realising that an increase in the number of two-seaters in the frontline would not yield such results, priority was placed on the continued development of single-seat fighters, which by August 1916 saw them concentrated in pursuit squadrons called *Jagdstaffeln* (Hunting Squadrons, or *Jastas*). This organisation of single-seaters allowed them to be rapidly deployed at decisive points along the front, and they were to assume the primary role in the quest for aerial supremacy.

In his post-war memoir *Germany's War in the Air*, von Hoeppner wrote the following about German aviators, although it also applies to their English and French counterparts:

> These men, for the most part young, were enthused with an ardour as unique as their mission was special in its nature. When you fly at altitudes where the lungs need the assistance of oxygen, when you see above you and around you tanks filled with a highly inflammable substance, when you feel yourself carried along amid bursting shells by a motor of more than 100 horsepower, with its roar deadening the human voice, you must agree that pilot and observer need a peculiar type of courage in handling the stick, machine gun, bomb release, camera or wireless key.
>
> As his encouragement in combat, the aviator does not have the example of his leader who goes before him or the shouts of comrades by his side. All he has to sustain him is the unswerving devotion to duty. He exposes his life daily, by his own volition in the absence of all direction and with the knowledge that in the moment of danger he must depend on himself alone. To meet the requirements of the air you need nerves of steel and youth's scorn of danger, together with a deep sense of responsibility. Looked at from the ground this may seem caused by unreasoning carelessness, but it finds justification in the optimistic bravery of the man who is always ready to sacrifice his life.

COMBAT

By the time the Albatros D I/II entered the arena of Western Front aerial combat in late August/early September 1916, the DH 2 had already been flying and fighting there for more than six months. During the first of these months No. 24 Sqn had shouldered the DH 2's load alone, escorting two-seater reconnaissance aeroplanes as a result of dangers imposed by the E III 'Fokker Scourge'. Inevitably, such missions brought the DH 2 into conflict with the dreaded German machine, but soon the British pushers, and the men who flew them, began making names for themselves.

For example, on 25 April No. 24 Sqn DH 2s escorting BE 2cs from No. 15 Sqn were set upon by a flight of Eindeckers, one of which was piloted by the great German ace Oblt Max Immelmann. Having initially seen action at the controls of LVG two-seaters with *FFA* 10 and then *FFA* 62, Immelmann had begun flying the unit's single-seat Eindeckers in 1915. He soon gained a reputation for being an aggressive fighter pilot, shooting down a then incredible eight aeroplanes by mid-January 1916 to win the *Orden Pour le Mérite*. On the prowl on 25 April for victory number 15, Immelmann spotted British machines some 700m (2,297ft) above him and attacked them, despite his altitude disadvantage. However, things did not develop as the great ace had anticipated:

> I came up and attacked one. He seemed to heel over after a few shots, but unfortunately I was mistaken. The two worked splendidly together in the course of the fight and put 11 shots into my machine. The petrol tank, the struts on the fuselage, the undercarriage and the propeller were hit. I could only save myself by a nose-dive of 1,000 metres [3,280ft].

He had engaged DH 2s flown by Lt N. P. Manfield and 2Lt J. O. Andrews, the latter of whom would be involved in one of the war's most legendary aerial battles in

Classic shot of No. 24 Sqn DH 2s lined up at Bertangles in July 1916. Note the Morane-Saulnier Type N at far right. (Jon Guttman)

the coming autumn, as will be seen. The result of their actions against Immelmann supplied an enormous confidence boost to the pilots of No. 24 Sqn. They had met the dreaded Fokker Eindecker and it had been theirs.

No. 29 Sqn DH 2s had joined the fray just prior to this pivotal encounter, arriving at Abeele, on the French/Belgian border, on 15 April. Yet things were relatively quiet for the unit initially since, according to future 32-victory ace 2Lt Geoffrey Hilton Bowman, 'we were in the Ypres Salient and all the Huns had gone down to the Somme'. Squadronmate and future 57-victory ace Flt Sgt James McCudden concurred that German machines were 'quite inactive' throughout the summer, and he believed this was due to the particularly accurate German anti-aircraft (AA) defences that No. 29 Sqn encountered:

Ground personnel manhandle a DH 2 into its hangar at Abeele, circa May 1916. Note the pole-mounted hangar windsock and replacement aileron on the machine at left. (Alex Revell)

We, on DH 2s at 12000ft, were very slow, and when we crossed the lines at all we always went through a devil of a hot show. Several enemy AA sections earned themselves my never ending respect, notably one gunner at Bixschoot, one at Passchendaele, one at Houthem and another near Fromelles. I have always had the utmost admiration for the enemy AA defences from the sea to La Bassée during the summer months of 1916, for they largely helped the enemy to employ his main aerial forces farther south where they were urgently needed.

No. 32 Sqn's Capt Herman von Poellnitz beats up Vert Galand in the summer of 1916. The aeroplane boasts interplane strut streamers and 'C' Flight markings on the wheel covers. (Aaron Weaver)

No. 29 Sqn was not totally devoid of German fighter opposition, however, as on 14 July 2Lt Brearley attacked and claimed a 'monoplane, light brown colour, black crosses on white background, believed to be a Fokker' while escorting a bombing sortie to Westroosbeke. Brearley's combat report stated that after a diving attack at 5000ft, in which he fired only six shots, the German machine 'fell sideways and then nose-dived into the ground'.

Further south, No. 32 Sqn arrived in-country on 7 June at Treizennes, commanded by six-victory ace Capt Lionel Wilmot Brabazon Rees. Commissioned in the Royal Garrison Artillery in 1903, Rees was attached to the West African Frontier Force until seconded to the RFC on 10 August 1914. An aggressive pilot who flew the FB 5 Gunbus with No. 11 Sqn, Rees had been credited with six victories, five of which were with observer Flt Sgt J. M. Hargreaves, by 6 October 1915. These successes made them the war's only Gunbus aces.

Rees assumed command of No. 32 Sqn the following year, and although an RFC directive forbade squadron commanders from flying combat sorties, he did so whenever possible. Thus on the first day of the Somme offensive – 1 July 1916 – Rees and Lt J. C. Simpson took off at 0555 hrs from Treizennes to patrol between La Bassée, Loos and Souchez. While Rees searched for returning British bombers Simpson spotted ten German two-seaters from *Kagohl* 3 *Kasta* 14 and attacked them alone. However, concentrated German return fire struck Simpson in the head and killed him, sending his DH 2 crashing into the Loos canal below.

Rees had also spotted the German formation by then, although he mistook them for the expected British bombers. As he approached them he was attacked by a diving aeroplane that he chased off with return fire. Turning his attention to an LFG Roland C II *Walfisch* (Whale), Rees peppered it with 30 rounds until 'a big cloud of blue haze came out of the nacelle in front of the pilot'. Returning to the now scattered German formation, Rees shot down two *Walfischen* before he was hit in the leg by a shot from below. Regardless of his wounded leg's intermittent paralysis, he attacked another *Walfisch* with a full drum of ammunition and then attempted to shoot at it with his pistol, but the Roland outpaced the DH 2 so Rees disengaged and flew back to Treizennes, leaving the once disciplined formation of German bombers 'scattered in twos and ones all over the sky'. Having landed safely, Rees climbed out of his DH 2, sat on the grass 'and calmly told the fellows to bring him a tender to take him to hospital'.

About his commander, 2Lt Gwilym H. Lewis opined:

> Of course, everyone knows the Major is mad. I don't think he was ever more happy in his life than attacking those Huns. He said he would have brought them all down one after the other if he could have used his leg.

Rees was credited with a *Walfisch* sent down out of control and another forced to land, and for his actions that day he received the Victoria Cross (VC).

Back at No. 24 Sqn, commander Hawker's 'ATTACK EVERYTHING' directive reverberated throughout the unit, and on 21 July a DH 2 patrol happened upon five *Walfischen* near Roisel, escorted by five Eindeckers. During the subsequent combat Andrews shot down a Fokker, which he saw execute a hard forced landing that sheared off its undercarriage, after which Andrews dived down and strafed a group of Germans approaching the fallen machine.

It is believed that Andrews' opponent was eight-victory ace and *Orden Pour le Mérite* winner Ltn Otto Parschau, commander of *Abwehrkommando Nord* (Defence Command North). Yet another pilot to come to the Eindecker after first serving with reconnaissance units (in this case *FFA 42*, *FFA 261* and *Brieftauben-Abteilung- Ostende* (Carrier Pigeon Section)) in 1915, Parschau had been credited with downing six two-seaters and two observation balloons by 9 July 1916. Mortally wounded in the head and chest during the action of the 21st, he managed to reach the ground safely and receive medical attention, only to succumb to his wounds during an operation that evening.

Although credited to Andrews, who was flying DH 2 5948, the precise time of Parschau's downing is unknown, creating uncertainty regarding the identity of his victor. Some historians suggest that it may have been the celebrated and colourful French ace Lt Charles Nungesser. In any event, the East Prussian's death was the second to befall an *Orden Pour le Mérite* decorated aviator (Immelmann being the first, having been killed on 18 June fighting FE 2bs of No. 25 Sqn) that summer. As Greg VanWyngarden wrote in *Osprey Aircraft of the Aces 73 – Early German Aces of World War 1*, 'Parschau's death placed another exclamation point on the end of any semblance of German control of the air over the Somme.'

Fortunately for the Germans, their salvation was not long in coming. Pre-production Albatros D I and D II machines were already being tested and refined at Johannisthal, and in August the first *Jagdstaffeln* were formed from the pilots and aeroplanes of the *Kampfeinsitzer-Kommandos* (single-seat fighter detachments, or *KEKs*). The *Jastas* would employ 14 new D-type fighters on a

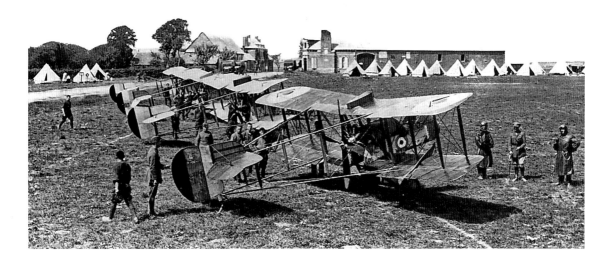

two-fold mission. First, seek and destroy enemy fighters to protect German army cooperation two-seater reconnaissance aeroplanes from interruption and molestation, and second, seek out and destroy enemy two-seater reconnaissance and artillery spotting aeroplanes.

Thus, Hptm Oswald Boelcke – *Orden Pour le Mérite* decorated and Germany's leading ace with 19 victories, who had been sent away on a tour of the Balkans after the 18 June death of Immelmann – was recalled to the Western Front and tasked with assembling the second *Jagdstaffel, Jasta* 2. At least partly comprised of eager single-seat fighter neophytes that Boelcke hand-selected from various two-seater units, *Jasta* 2 had been formed approximately three weeks before the availability of its share of new Albatros D I/IIs. Thus Boelcke flew 'lone wolf' patrols with a rotary-engined Fokker D III and shot down eight more aeroplanes – including three DH 2s – until at last the new Albatros Ds began arriving at *Jasta* 2 on 16 September. These new machines were immediately beloved by the *Jagdstaffelpiloten*, including Ltn Erwin Böhme:

Our new machines likewise border on marvellous. They are far improved over the single-seaters we flew at Verdun. Their climb rate and manoeuvrability are astonishing – it is as if they were living, feeling beings that understood what their master wishes. With them, one can dare and achieve everything.

Thereafter *Jasta* 2 flew multi-aeroplane patrols, the presence and impact of which were noted immediately by the RFC. As per their purpose, the pilots of *Jasta* 2 preyed upon many BE 2c, Sopwith 1½ Strutter and FE 2b two-seaters, but inevitably the Albatros D I/IIs and DH 2s found themselves duelling as well.

The early contacts ended in stalemates, such as on 15 September when a flight of three DH 2s from No. 24 Sqn 'attacked two HA approaching our lines from the Bapaume–Peronne road. One machine went down vertically for 1,000ft then side-slipped and flattened out. A small single-seater scout continually attacked, and owing to its superior speed and climb, could not be continually engaged.'

Fellow Osprey author Greg VanWyngarden has ascertained that this captured machine is DH 2 7873 of No. 24 Sqn, seen here on 14 September 1916 after becoming *Jasta* 2 *Staffelführer* Oswald Boelcke's 24th victory. Although still two days before the bulk of the unit's Albatros Ds arrived, the duel between *Jasta* 2 and No. 24 Sqn was already underway. Note 7873's white/blue/red rudder stripes. (Greg VanWyngarden)

Soon the encounters became bloodier, such as on 16 October when Boelcke attacked a No. 24 Sqn DH 2 flown by 'C' Flight commander and ten-victory ace Lt P.A. Langan-Byrne, who was on an Offensive Patrol with several other DH 2s. Boelcke wrote that at 1745 hrs he spotted the 'C' Flight pushers and 'went into some fine turns. The English leader, with streamers on his machine, came just right for me. I settled him with my first attack – apparently the pilot was killed, for the machine spun down. I watched it down until it crashed about a kilometre east of Beaulencourt'. It was Boelcke's 34th victory overall, and his 15th since *Jasta* 2's formation six weeks previously.

Boelcke's skill and leadership had a profound effect on the *Staffel*, and its morale soared. 'It is somewhat unique how Boelcke conveys his spirit to each and every one

DH 2 7873 is inspected by *Jasta* 2 pilots Otto Höhne (in cockpit), Oswald Boelcke (centre) and Manfred von Richthofen (right).

of his students, how he carries them all away,' wrote Böhme. 'They follow him wherever he leads. Not one would leave him in the lurch! He is a born leader! No wonder that his *Staffel* blossoms!' Future 80-victory ace and *Orden Pour le Mérite* decorated Manfred von Richthofen, then a leutnant with *Jasta* 2, had similar sentiments, writing retrospectively:

It was a wonderful time at our squadron. The spirit of the leader spread to his pupils. We could blindly trust his leadership. There was no possibility that anyone would be left behind. The thought never came to us. And so we roamed bright and merry, diminishing our enemies.

On Saturday, 28 October, Boelcke and his *Staffelkamerad*, and personal friend, Böhme had just sat down to enjoy a game of chess when *Jasta* 2 'were called shortly after four o'clock during an infantry attack on the front'. Boelcke had flown several sorties already that day, but he led his *Staffel* of Albatros D Is and D IIs aloft again into the cloudy, stormy skies. Ltn von Richthofen recalled that eventually, while flying at about 10,000ft between Pozières and Flers, 'from a great distance we saw two imprudent Englishmen over the Front, apparently having fun in the bad weather'.

The tattered remains of No. 24 Sqn DH 2 A2542, which was being flown by Lt P. A. Langan-Byrne when he was shot down on 16 October 1916 by Oswald Boelcke for his 34th victory. This unusual angle affords a good view of the Gnome Monosoupape engine, wing attachment points and the four-bladed, brass-sheathed propeller. (Greg VanWyngarden)

These two aeroplanes were No. 24 Sqn 'C' Flight DH 2s flown by six-victory ace Lt Arthur Gerald Knight (A2594) and Lt Alfred Edwin McKay (A2554), performing a northeast–southwest defensive patrol between Pozières and Bapaume. At 8,500ft, Knight was about 1,500ft higher than McKay, whose departure from Bertangles had been delayed 'on account of [a] dud engine', forcing him to take a second machine aloft that he noted 'would not climb' – typical examples of the engine woes often faced by No. 24 Sqn. At about 1640 hrs the pair spotted *Jasta* 2's Albatrosses and identified them as 'Halberstadters and small Aviatic [sic] Scouts', who stalked them for five minutes until one 'did a side-slipping dive under the top DH, but Lt Knight did not attack, as he was suspicious of this manoeuvre'.

As the leader, it is likely that this attacking aeroplane was Boelcke, who according to von Richthofen 'went after one and I the other'. Knight wrote that he was initially attacked by six of the twelve aeroplanes and immediately commenced evasive spiralling before the other six attacked, some of whom went down below him and attacked McKay as well. Outnumbered six-to-one, the DH 2s could do little amidst the swirling cloud of German fighters. 'It would have been fatal to concentrate on any one machine as four or five [others] were ready to close in', wrote Knight, 'so I merely spiralled and fired when a HA came across my sights'.

The same opinion was held by Böhme, who in a letter to his fiancée wrote that 'the English aircraft, fast single-seaters, skilfully defended themselves' during a 'wildly gyrating melée in which we could always only get into range for brief moments'.

Oswald Boelcke suited for flight as his Albatros D II D.386/16 warms up behind him in the autumn of 1916. An average temperature lapse rate of 3.5 degrees per 1,000ft meant that on even mild autumn days pilots faced near zero degree temperatures at combat altitude.

No doubt the sheer number of German aeroplanes chasing the same two targets crowded the airspace, aiding the British and threatening to violate Boelcke's eighth dictum that cautioned against several fighters pursuing the same opponent, although perhaps there was little choice in so lopsided a battle. Regardless, the threat proved all too real.

After 'about five minutes of strenuous fighting', during which *Jasta* 2 'attempted to force our opponents downward by alternately blocking their path, as we had previously so often done with success', Boelcke and Böhme were pursuing McKay when Knight, under attack by von Richthofen, turned hard left to evade and cut in front of McKay's pursuers. Both Germans manoeuvered to avoid colliding with the DH 2 but tragically hit each other instead, each Albatros having been in the blind spot of the other.

Böhme's undercarriage struck Boelcke's upper port wing, and although the impact was described as a 'light touch', Böhme lost part of his undercarriage and the outboard section of Boelcke's wing was torn away. 'How can I describe my feelings from that moment on', Böhme later wrote, 'when Boelcke suddenly appeared just a few metres to my right, how he dived, how I jerked upward [after each had become aware of their too-close proximity], and how we nevertheless grazed each other, and both plummeted downward!'

Böhme fell 200m (656ft) but recovered to follow Boelcke's crippled D II, gliding left-wing-low 'in great spiralling curves' toward the clouds. His description of this descent suggests that Boelcke had also lost his port aileron, which would reduce or eliminate use of the starboard aileron – or if the starboard aileron still functioned, it was not enough to fully arrest the roll caused by the now asymmetrical lift created by

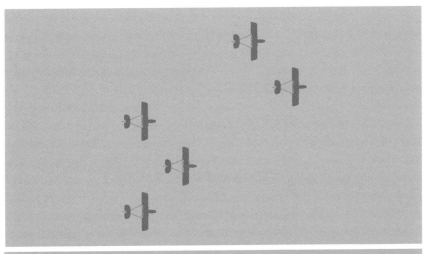

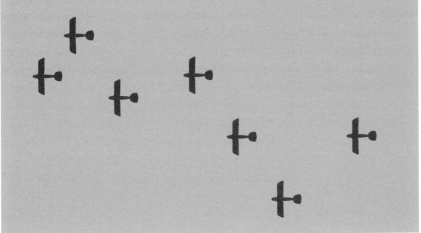

the partly missing wing. Ltn von Richthofen wrote that he followed Boelcke as well, at least initially, and his account agreed with Böhme's that Boelcke descended from the fight while under some control. Knight and McKay also saw Boelcke's initial descent and concurred his Albatros was under control.

However, he entered a lower layer of clouds (in which one encounters increased turbulence) and thence according to von Richthofen lost his entire upper wing. Böhme observed that Boelcke 'went into an ever steepening glide, and I saw before the landing how he could no longer keep his aeroplane facing straightforward, and how he struck the ground near a gun battery'.

Böhme attempted to land near the crash site but was thwarted by the surrounding shell holes and trenches, and he was forced to return to *Jasta* 2's base at Lagnicourt. His damaged undercarriage caused his Albatros to nose over on landing. Unhurt, he and several others drove back to the crash site with stolen hopes of Boelcke's survival, but these were dashed by the grim reality of his corpse that the adjacent gun crew had extricated from the wreckage. Böhme opined the crash might have been survivable had Boelcke worn a crash helmet (something not usually done by *Jagdstaffelpiloten*) and had strapped himself firmly into his D II, which might have better protected him from the blunt-force trauma that fractured his skull and killed him. In any event, the great 40-victory ace was dead.

That night, Boelcke's brother Wilhelm sent a telegram to their sister – 'Prepare parents. Oswald mortally injured today over German lines'.

McKay and Knight had continued their swirling battle against the rest of *Jasta 2* for another 15 minutes after the collision, each DH 2 having descended to 5,000ft and drifted east of Bapaume. Finally, the Albatrosses disengaged to the east and the British scouts returned to Bertangles, where they landed safely at 1740 hrs. By the time *Jasta 2* returned en masse to Lagnicourt, word of Boelcke's death had already reached the aerodrome. Naturally, the pilots – indeed, soon the entire *Luftstreitkräfte* – were shocked. 'One could hardly conceive of it,' recalled von Richthofen.

On 31 October Boelcke's body was borne to Cambrai Cathedral for an elaborate funeral service. Afterwards, the coffin was taken via gun carriage to the train station and transported back to his home town of Dessau, in Germany, where he was buried on 2 November after a funeral attended by family, high-ranking generals and royalty.

A photograph of him lying in state under a blanket of autumn oak leaves and flowers reveals little head trauma, save for cranial disfigurement near his left temple and eye, perhaps lending some credence to Böhme's opinion of the survivability of Boelcke's crash. However, a purported witness to the crash claimed Boelcke's D II overturned on landing and caused a mortal wound to the back of his head, which would likely require the complete collapse of the centre section struts. In the absence of photographs or descriptions of the wreck, such detail is speculative at best.

No. 24 Sqn DH 2 5998 at Bertangles, showing off its sawtooth nacelle pattern and red-and-white banded interplane struts. Capt John Andrews was flying this machine when he participated in the shooting down of *Jasta 2 Staffelführer* Oblt Stefan Kirmaier for his seventh victory. (Aaron Weaver)

After Boelcke's death, seven-victory ace Oblt Stefan Kirmaier was appointed *Staffelführer* of *Jasta* 2 on 30 October. Born on 28 July 1889 at Lachen, Kirmaier had served with the 8th Infantry Regiment until his transfer into the *Fliegertruppe*, where he flew with *FA(A)* 203 in 1915–16 before his attachment to *KEK* Jametz, with whom he scored three victories. Joining *Jasta* 2 in early October, Kirmaier served under Boelcke and downed another four aeroplanes prior to his assumption of command.

On 13 November the last thrust of the Somme offensive began with the Battle of the Ancre. Four days later Kirmaier led *Jasta* 2 in a clash with their RFC rivals No. 24 Sqn, which lost a DH 2 to Ltn Höhne's guns, killing 2Lt W. C. Crawford. On the 22nd Kirmaier led *Jasta* 2 over the lines west of Bapaume, where they claimed a No. 3 Sqn Morane Parasol (Böhme's seventh victory) and shot down a No. 11 Sqn FE 2b (König's second victory). However, several No. 24 Sqn DH 2s were in the area, many of whom saw the Parasol falling (which, in actuality, was able to regain the lines and limp home with a wounded crew).

There are variations as to what transpired next, but according to the No. 24 Sqn Record Book, Capt Andrews (who had become Temporary Captain on 30 April) and Lt K. Crawford reported 'several HA dived' at them. Andrews claimed they did not fire at him, and he was able to fasten onto the tail of the lowest machine and 'fired about ten rounds when he tried to jink and then fell out of control'. Meanwhile, Crawford wrote that after he 'got on one HA's tail and fired half a drum, he nose-dived', after which he 'saw Capt Andrews just above me' – ostensibly both men were attacking the same Albatros.

Böhme's recollection of events was 'five of us were underway and we were attacked by two big squadrons at the same time over there. Each of us had to handle several opponents. I saw Kirmaier as he hotly pursued a Vickers two-seater, but had several behind him.'

Despite these account discrepancies, it was indeed Kirmaier who had attracted the attention of Andrews and Crawford, whose DH 2s now pursued the stricken Albatros into the thick ground mist below. Andrews continued firing until he lost sight of Kirmaier in the reduced visibility, but 'could follow the smoke trail made by his engine' and eventually discovered that the machine had crashed between Les Boeufs and Le Transloy. Crawford and Andrews circled 1,500ft above the wreckage, but when they turned for home Crawford's 'engine conked' and he was forced to land 2,000 yards south of Guedecourt and 1,500 yards east of Flers. Securing his DH 2, Crawford met up with a major from the 3rd Australian Trench Mortar Battery and walked back to the wreckage of Kirmaier's D II:

Found Hun machine at N.28a central. Pilot was killed, shot through the back. Machine was a single-seater with *ALBATROSS* [sic] on his tail. The engine was buried beneath

Oblt Stefan Kirmaier had three victories when he arrived at *Jasta* 2 from *Kek* Jametz on 5 October 1916, and he was credited with eight more – including a DH 2 on 26 October – prior to being shot down and killed by No. 24 Sqn DH 2s on 22 November 1916. (Collection DEHLA)

No. 24 Sqn and RFC luminary Maj Lanoe Hawker VC. A gifted pilot, instructor, leader and inventor of everything from clothing to gunsights, his 'Attack Everything' mantra contributed much towards RFC aerial domination in the summer of 1916. Following his demise in combat on 23 November 1916, fellow No. 24 Sqn ace Capt John Andrews noted 'Lanoe Hawker's death came as a great blow as everyone liked him, and had absolute confidence in him as a commanding officer'. DH 2 ace and squadronmate Capt Robert Saundby quoted Shakespeare when describing Maj Hawker. 'His life was gentle, and the elements so mixed in him that Nature might stand up and say to all the world, "This was a man".'

the ground. He had two machine guns fixed one either side of his engine, each with a 500-round belt. These guns were taken by Gen Elliot of the 15th Australian Infantry Brigade in a damaged condition.

In retrospect it seems the popular account of Kirmaier having been surprised while leading neophytes on a tour of the lines is erroneous, and the oft-reported 'back of the head' mortal wound location is at odds with Crawford's observation of Kirmaier's body, but in any event the 27-year-old ace was dead. *Jasta* 2 had lost its second *Staffelführer* in a month during conflicts with No. 24 Sqn DH 2s, yet the following day it would rush the net with a mortal volley that led to one of the war's most epic, yet misunderstood, duels.

At 1300 hrs (British time) on 14 November four No. 24 Sqn 'A' Flight DH 2s left Bertangles aerodrome on a defensive patrol of the British 4th Army front near Bapaume. Leading this quartet was 'A' Flight commander Andrews, accompanied by Capt Robert Henry Magnus Spencer Saundby, 2Lt John Henry Crutch and, as a last-minute replacement, No. 24 Sqn CO Maj Lanoe George Hawker VC DSO.

ENGAGING THE ENEMY

Gunsights on the DH 2 and Albatros scouts were very simple affairs. The DH 2 employed a rear sight that could be swung vertically to sight over the circular ammunition drum, while the Albatros scouts employed ring and bead sights, although with both aeroplanes there were occasional machines outfitted with tubular Aldis sights. No. 24 Sqn CO and part-time inventor Lanoe Hawker experimented with various sights designed to aid deflection shooting, but it is without question that gunsights were not as important for shooting down an enemy as was attaining the closest range possible before opening fire. Firing within a few aeroplane lengths obviated the need for a telescopic gunsight and maximised the damaging effects of bullet strikes, since rounds lose less energy over shorter distances than they do over longer distances.

Shortly before his death, Manfred von Richthofen wrote an Air Combat Operations Manual that stated, in part, 'With one sentence one can settle the topic "Air Combat Tactics". Namely, "I go up to within 50 metres of the enemy from behind, aim cleanly, then the opponent falls." These are the words with which Boelcke served me when I asked him his trick. Now I know that is the whole secret of shooting them

down. One does not need to be a flight artist or a marksman but only to have the courage to fly right up to the opponent.'

Furthermore, attacking with surprise greatly increased a pilot's chances of success and survival. It mattered not at all if an enemy aeroplane was more manoeuvrable or better armed if it could be brought down unawares before its advantages could be utilised. However, 'If [an enemy pilot] has been watchful', continued von Richthofen, 'he immediately begins to turn [the beginnings of a dogfight] at which point one endeavoured to make tight turns and to stay above the opponent'. Although he disbelieved in attacking two-seaters from head-on, there were occasions when he attacked single-seaters in such a way. Nevertheless, he believed success via this methodology was rare.

Case in point was 27 December 1916, when von Richthofen executed a head-on attack against a DH 2 believed to be flown by James McCudden, as depicted here. Both men fired but a jammed gun forced McCudden to spin away. Although von Richthofen pursued him until they were at low altitude, he was forced to disengage due to anti-aircraft fire. Later, McCudden wrote that during this encounter his machine had not been hit.

Jasta 2 pilots in an informal moment at Lagnicourt. They are, from left to right, Oblt Stefan Kirmaier (*Staffelführer*) and Ltns Hans Imelmann, Manfred von Richthofen and Hans Wortmann. The presence of Kirmaier (killed in action on 22 November 1916) and Wortmann (who had arrived at *Jasta* 2 by at least 9 November) together dates the photograph as having been taken within the first three weeks of November.

Born on 30 December 1890 in Longparish, Hampshire, Hawker was an accomplished pilot of considerable experience. Having flown reconnaissance sorties with No. 6 Sqn during the early war, Hawker flew a solo BE 2c bombing mission against the Gontrode Zeppelin sheds near Ghent, in Belgium, on 19 April 1915 – an action for which he was subsequently awarded the Distinguished Service Order (DSO). As the war progressed he flew reconnaissance sorties in FE 2bs, with one observer commenting that Hawker 'had a foul habit of carrying an ordinary rifle which he used to loose off if he didn't think I was doing too well [shooting at German aeroplanes]. The noise just over my head was most alarming, and annoying'.

Later Hawker acquired a single-seat Bristol Scout and rigged it with a fuselage-mounted machine gun that fired obliquely outside the propeller arc. With his aeroplane so equipped, Hawker attacked and received credit for downing two Albatros C-type two-seaters on 25 July 1915. One of his victims 'burst into flames and turned upside down, the observer falling out. The machine and pilot crashed to earth'. Hawker received the VC for these two victories, thus becoming the first RFC scout pilot so decorated. During the following month Hawker claimed three additional victories, and upon returning to England on 20 September his victory tally stood at seven (three in the FE 2b and four in the Bristol Scout).

Eight days later Hawker assumed command of No. 24 Sqn, a weeks-old unit with which he spent the next four months training pilots on various two-seaters. Eventually re-equipped with DH 2s, the unit departed for France on 7 February 1916, thus becoming the first solely equipped single-seater squadron to proceed to a combat zone. On 10 February it established residence at Bertangles, whereupon 'war-flying proper immediately commenced'.

Like Capt L. W. B. Rees at No. 32 Sqn, Hawker's command responsibilities precluded his mission participation, which eroded his combat currency. Nevertheless, he made efforts to accompany his pilots whenever the pilot pool was low or, as was the reason for his participation with 'A' Flight's sortie on 23 November, there was a 'young pilot about to go on leave' in whose slot the altruistic Hawker occupied lest misfortune befall an aviator so close to a well-earned respite.

On his last sortie Hawker followed Andrews through clear skies dominated by high pressure. 'A' Flight's ingress was uneventful until 1330 hrs, when its pilots spotted a 'rough house going on over Grandcourt' between No. 60 Sqn Nieuports and unidentified 'HA'. 'A' Flight power-dived to join the fight but arrived after the Nieuports had driven away most of the German aeroplanes. Crutch saw Hawker 'go N[orth] after [a] single seater HA' and began following, but his engine, already running roughly for at least part, if not all, of the flight, 'cut out on two cylinders and started to knock', necessitating his precautionary landing at No. 9 Sqn's airfield near Morlancourt. There, Crutch discovered 'two plugs damaged and tappet rods out of adjustment' – maladies all-too-common with DH 2 7919, an aeroplane plagued with sundry engine malfunctions.

Andrews, Saundby and Hawker continued inbound until shortly after 1350 hrs when, near Achiet, the former spotted two German two-seaters flying at 6,000ft northeast of Bapaume and immediately led 'A' Flight into a diving attack that 'drove them [the Germans] east'. During this chase Andrews scanned his surrounding airspace and discovered 'two strong patrols of HA scouts above me'. He realised that a long pursuit of the eastward-fleeing Germans was imprudent in the face of such a threat and thus broke off his attack, but 'a DH Scout, [flown by] Maj Hawker, dived past me and continued to pursue'. Not wanting to abandon Hawker, who was ostensibly unaware of the German scouts above him, Andrews and Saundby followed him eastward and 'were at once attacked by the HA, one of which dived onto Maj Hawker's tail'.

These attacking scouts were *Jasta* 2 Albatros D IIs (and likely D Is) led by Ltn von Richthofen, now de facto *Jasta* 2 *Staffelführer* in the wake of Kirmaier's death the previous day. Although known worldwide today as 'The Red Baron', in November 1916 von Richthofen was still an up-and-coming fighter pilot who less than three months prior had been among those hand-selected by Boelcke to join the newly formed *Jasta* 2.

Born on 2 May 1892 in Breslau, Silesia, von Richthofen entered a military academy in 1909 and upon graduation was assigned to the 1st Uhlan Regiment. When war began he served on the Eastern and Western fronts, but became bored with trench warfare and transferred into the *Fliegertruppe* as an observer, serving several months in that capacity until learning to fly and attaining his pilot certificate on Christmas Day, 1915. Flying a two-seater on reconnaissance and bombing sorties on both fronts, von Richthofen eventually rigged a machine gun to a LFG Roland C II and shot down a Nieuport scout, although this victory remained unconfirmed and was therefore not part of his credited victory list.

OVERLEAF
On 23 November 1916 Ltn Manfred von Richthofen led Ltn Dieter Collin and several other *Jasta* 2 pilots in a diving attack against three No. 24 Sqn DH 2s. Outnumbering the RFC machines and using their height advantage to its fullest extent, the Albatros D Is and D IIs tore into the trio of DH 2s and ultimately shot down two of them.

No. 24 Sqn Flight leader Capt John Andrews wrote, 'I was about to abandon the pursuit [of the two-seaters] when a DH Scout, [flown by] Maj Hawker, dived past me and continued to pursue'. After the Albatrosses fell on them, Andrews had his DH 2 'badly shot about. Large hole in cambox of engine, also one cylinder shot through, smashed piston, etc.' Gliding toward the lines, his salvation arrived in the form of the trio's third pilot, Capt Robert Saundby, who dived onto the attacking Albatros and 'emptied three-quarters double drum [72 bullets] into him at about 20 yards' range', forcing him into a diving escape that Saundby believed led to a crash. Although he received credit for an 'out of control', there were no *Jasta* 2 losses or forced landings.

Meanwhile, Maj Lanoe Hawker VC and von Richthofen became embroiled in a descending turn fight that drifted deeper into German territory, and upon making a break for British lines Hawker was shot and killed, becoming von Richthofen's first DH 2 victory and 11th victim overall.

63

MARK POSTLETHWAITE

A close-cropped Ltn Manfred von Richthofen in his 'dirty, oily, leather flying jacket'. He was credited with shooting down five DH 2s in his career, four while flying Albatros D IIs in *Jasta* 2.

His selection by Boelcke to join *Jasta* 2 proved to be a sage choice, for within nine weeks of shooting down his first confirmed aeroplane von Richthofen had already accrued nine additional victories – a tally greater than any of the other *Jasta* 2 'first team' pilots, five of whom had been killed by 23 November.

As *Jasta* 2 dived on 'A' Flight, the RFC pilots found themselves involved in what Saundby's logbook described as a 'violent fight'. Two Albatrosses attacked his DH 2, forcing him to spiral 'two or three times' before the Germans disengaged and 'zoomed off'. Andrews went after the Albatros attacking Hawker and 'drove him off, firing about 25 rounds at close range', but in the process was attacked by a fourth Albatros. Its accurate gunfire struck the DH 2's engine, incapacitating it and forcing a glide with which Andrews was 'obliged to try to regain our lines'. The pursuing German pilot fired continually, his astute gunnery reflected by Andrew's logbook entry – 'Machine badly shot about. Large hole in cambox of engine, also one cylinder shot through, smashed piston, etc.'

Fortunately for Andrews, Saundby found himself in a good position to attack this belligerent and fired 'three-quarters of a double drum into him at about 20 yards' range', after which the Albatros 'wobbled' and then power-dived away. Saundby went after him, but the Albatros out-dived his DH 2 and he could not follow. However, this attack had saved Andrews from further molestation as he glided away.

Pulling level, Saundby assessed the situation and saw that the German aeroplanes had moved away to the east. Although he saw Andrews nearby, there was no sign of Hawker. Andrews last saw Hawker 'at about 3,000ft near Bapaume, fighting with an HA apparently quite under control but going down', at which point he had had to break visual contact so as to concentrate on his dead-stick approach and landing in Guillemont, which he executed successfully at 1410 hrs.

What Andrews had glimpsed was the approximate midpoint of the now legendary combat between Hawker and von Richthofen, which by Andrews' eyewitness account had developed into a continuous series of tight descending spirals. As von Richthofen's autobiography *Der Rote Kampfflieger* described, 'Thus we both turned like madmen in circles, with engines running full-throttle at 3,500 metres' [11,482ft] height. First 20 times left, then 30 times right, each mindful of getting above and behind the other.'

At 500m (1,640ft) Hawker ceased spiralling and began evasive aerobatics that involved 'looping and such tricks', after which he broke for the lines in a zig-zagging descent from 100m (328ft). His German opponent pursued him, firing steadily as his faster Albatros gained on the jinking DH 2, but at an altitude of just 30m (98ft) his guns jammed and 'almost cost me success'. Clearing his weapons, von Richthofen resumed firing until '50 metres [164ft] behind our lines' he saw Hawker's DH 2 begin an unchecked shallow descent and then impact the artillery-ravaged terrain near Ligny-Thilloy, one mile south of Bapaume. German soldiers who later inspected the wreck determined that Hawker had been shot once in the back of the head. He was buried next to his destroyed aeroplane, but ultimately his grave was lost in the turmoil of war.

As Immelmann's death had symbolically signified the end of the 'Fokker Scourge' and German aerial supremacy, Hawker's death signified the reclamation of German aerial supremacy.

But how had it happened? Although widely known amongst World War I aficionados, the tale of this epic battle is rife with frequent misconceptions that need addressing, such as the true length of the aces' spiralling fight. It is often said to have lasted '35 minutes' or a 'half-hour', but von Richthofen's combat report clearly states that 'after a long curve fight of 3–5 [three-to-five] minutes I had pressed my adversary down to 500 metres [1,640ft]'. Ignoring or overlooking the hyphen creates a subtle yet crucial and significant difference in time.

Another popular belief is that Hawker's defeat was the result of 'engine trouble' he experienced after the spiralling portion of the engagement, caused by his DH 2's Monosoupape engine running at full power during the entire 'half-hour' battle. However, as noted in the Technical Specifications chapter, the Monosoupape engine was either on or off no matter what the flight environment. When on, it ran at full power, whether engaged in turning combat for 30 minutes or flying over the English Channel for a 'half-hour'. Thus, there was no undue 'stress' imposed on the engine due to 'full revs in combat' because it was *always* at full revs. Furthermore, that the turning portion of the Hawker and von Richthofen fight lasted not a 'half-hour' but about five minutes renders the entire discussion moot.

No. 24 Sqn record books do reflect many instances of rough running engines or outright failures, as exemplified by Crutch's problems. They also reflect many instances when the engines ran well, as can be concluded from the absence of any mention of such trouble in Andrews' and Saundby's reports – and thus any speculation regarding engine performance must be considered both ways, good and bad. But if Hawker's engine performed as poorly as many contend it did, how was he able to execute low-altitude aerobatics (described by von Richthofen as 'looping and such tricks') between 500m (1,640ft) and 100m (328ft)? Low-altitude loops with a poorly running engine?

The contention of some that these loops and other aerobatics are what caused the engine to run poorly (for reasons never stated) are groundless. Hawker is the only person who could have reported the status of DH 2 5964's engine performance that day and, of course, he never returned to Bertangles to do so. Yet even with a perfectly running 100hp Monosoupape engine, a nearly year-old and war-worn DH 2 was not going to outrun a two-month-old 160hp Albatros D II, let alone one flown by the most tenacious and determined man in the whole of the *Luftstreitkräfte*.

Tactically, Hawker's defeat can be traced back to *Jasta* 2's initial attack, against which he did not defend himself. The reasons for this will never be known absolutely. While it is true Hawker's actions exemplified his 'attack everything' mantra, and thus he would have endeavoured to close the distance on the two-seaters that No. 24 Sqn spotted near Bapaume – which combat reports reveal that he did – it defies logic that such a combat veteran would have done so had he known Albatros fighters were raining down on him.

Andrews recognised the danger. He spotted the Albatrosses and immediately disengaged his pursuit of the two-seaters. Yet Hawker did not and carried on after them. Thus it passes speculation and enters a near certainty that Hawker had become fixated on the two-seaters, never saw *Jasta* 2's diving attack and likely never noticed Andrews break away, or at the very least did not recognise his reason for such a radical break from formation. From that moment on Hawker was in a position of disadvantage from which – although he fought gallantly – he could not recover.

Ltn von Richthofen's hard-fought victory over Hawker was the first of a series of four credited DH 2 successes he attained flying the Albatros D II through the remainder of 1916. The second of these victories came on 11 December when, just south of Arras at 1145 hrs, von Richthofen and Ltn d R Wortmann spotted No. 32 Sqn DH 2s escorting No. 23 Sqn FE 2bs on a bombing sortie. Singling out DH 2 5986, flown by three-victory 'B' Flight commander Lt B. P. G. Hunt, von Richthofen gave chase and 'after a short curve fight I ruined the adversary's motor and forced him to land behind our lines near Mercatel. Occupant not seriously wounded'. Indeed, Hunt was taken prisoner, but he had been wounded in the liver – ultimately he was involved in a prisoner exchange due to illness and held thereafter in neutral Holland until war's end.

Interestingly, Hunt's DH 2 had just been fitted with twin Lewis machine guns, and he had been out on his first sortie with his machine so equipped when he ran afoul of von Richthofen to become his 12th victory. Afterwards, DH 2 5986's rudder and engine placard were photographed amongst various items that von Richthofen had collected from his early victories.

Nine days later, von Richthofen was leading a five-Albatros *Jasta* 2 patrol at 3,000m (9,842ft) near Monchy-au-Bois when at 1130 hrs they tangled with No. 29 Sqn DH 2s out on an Offensive Patrol. After the initial clash the battle dissolved into a series of individual combats, and von Richthofen entered a turning battle with DH 2 7927 flown by 21-year-old eight-victory ace Capt A. G. Knight. Formerly with No. 24 Sqn, Knight had joined No. 29 Sqn the previous month. Whilst with his former unit, he had been the pilot von Richthofen had chased in front of Boelcke and Böhme to cause their mid-air collision the previous October.

Now finding himself being chased by von Richthofen again, Knight evaded the German ace until they had descended to 1,500m (4,921ft), where he was attacked 'at closest range (aeroplane length). I saw immediately that I had hit the enemy. First he went down in curves, then he dashed to the ground'. The German ace followed Knight down to within 100m (328ft) of the ground to verify his victory. In a further effort to secure the claim, he noted in his combat report that 'this aeroplane had only been attacked by me'. Knight, who had been killed either by aerial gunfire or the ensuing crash, became von Richthofen's 13th victim. As with Hunt's machine, pieces of 7927 entered the German's collection of souvenired trophies.

A little over two hours after his victory over Knight, von Richthofen led *Jasta* 2 on a subsequent patrol and downed another pusher, this time an FE 2b, for his 14th success. A week later, on 27 December, von Richthofen led a *Jasta* 2 patrol of five Albatrosses south of Arras and encountered No. 29 Sqn DH 2s, one of which was flown by then single-victory but future 57-victory ace Flt Sgt James McCudden, who recalled that after seeing 'five HA' he attacked an Albatros that had latched onto the tail of a DH 2 flown by Lt Jennings. This Albatros was von Richthofen's, who summarily disengaged and reversed course to attack McCudden head-on.

Although in his 1918 *Air Combat Operations Manual* von Richthofen opined that head-on attacks against two-seaters (which, as will be seen, he thought McCudden was flying) were 'very dangerous', in late 1916 he was still refining the lessons learned from

No. 29 Sqn's Flt Sgt James McCudden. Although 'Mac' achieved no Albatros D I or D II victories in DH 2s, he duelled future 'Red Baron' Manfred von Richthofen to a draw while flying the nimble pusher. Although von Richthofen received credit for the 'victory', McCudden lived on to down 57 aeroplanes in total prior to his death. (Alex Revell)

Boelcke, and ostensibly had not compiled enough experience to conclude the tactical ineffectiveness of this attack methodology. In January 1917 (by then flying the new Albatros D III) he was still experimenting with head-on attacks, such as when he encountered No. 40 Sqn FE 8s on the 23rd and attacked future ace Lt E. L. Benbow, who dived away and escaped.

Much the same result was had initially by McCudden, who wrote:

> This Hun at once came for me nose on, and we both fired simultaneously [his combat report stated 'from 100 yards'], but after firing about 20 shots [his combat report stated eight] my gun got a bad double feed, which I could not rectify at the time as I was now in the middle of five D I Albatrosses, so I half-rolled.

However, in this instance von Richthofen gave chase, so that when McCudden recovered and pulled level '"cack, cack, cack, cack" came from just behind me, and on looking round I saw my old friend with the black and white streamers again. I immediately half-rolled again, but still the Hun stayed there'. The tenacious von Richthofen pursued the fleeing McCudden in this manner until they were one mile over the lines in English territory, at which point hostile AA fire forced the German to disengage at 800ft and turn east for his lines. Finally free from pursuit McCudden rectified his jammed gun and turned his DH 2 after the retreating Albatros, but 'by this time the Hun was much higher, and very soon joined his patrol, who were waiting for him at about 5,000ft over Ransart'.

Mistakenly, von Richthofen claimed he had chased 'a very courageously flown Vickers two-seater' (referring to the FE 2b, a pusher that resembled a DH 2 but which was a larger two-seater) that 'crashed to the ground on the enemy side'. Clearly, McCudden had not crashed. In the frantic pace of their spinning combat it is easy to understand how von Richthofen misidentified his adversary's machine, and Air Batteries 13 and 47 were listed as corroborating witnesses to the 'victory' in his combat report. At the end of the day, however, McCudden's DH 2 had been 'chased absolutely out of the sky from 10,000ft to 800ft'. Although von Richthofen was duly given credit for his 15th, and last, victory of 1916, McCudden's survival proves that it was not a victory at all.

STATISTICS AND ANALYSIS

The window of Western Front *mano y mano* combat opportunity between the DH 2 and Albatros D I/II was brief. There were only three RFC squadrons equipped with DH 2s and the majority of their clashes with Albatrosses occurred during the 105 days between 17 September and 31 December 1916, after which the unusually severe winter conditions of early 1917 hampered combat sorties. This was also the period during which the quantity of Albatros D Is and D IIs began declining as new Albatros D IIIs started to arrive at the front in steady and increasing numbers.

Albatros victories credited to DH 2 pilots, and vice-versa, are very low when compared with similar duels between other aeroplane makes and models later in the war. Indeed, most of the pilots on either side credited with shooting down an Albatros D I/II or DH 2 retained that as their sole victory over the type. The ostentatious

The Albatros D II soldiered on into 1917, as seen here in this March view of *Jasta* 5's captured Albatros D II (OAW) D.910/16, flown by Ltn Max Böhme. The rough OAW camouflage colour demarcation is shown to good effect, as is the Garuda propeller. (Greg VanWyngarden)

A *Jasta* 16b Albatros D II in flight shows off its rugged yet graceful lines. (Collection DEHLA)

exception is Manfred von Richthofen, credited with shooting down four of his five DH 2s while flying Albatros D IIs in *Jasta* 2.

These low type-specific victory numbers may lead one astray to conclude that there was little aerial combat at that stage of the war, but one must consider that the primary mission of the *Jagdstaffeln* was to attack two-seater reconnaissance or bombing aeroplanes. During his time flying Albatros D IIs, *Jasta* 2 *Staffelführer* Oswald Boelcke had only a single DH 2 victory to his credit, but he also shot down 13 other aeroplanes, of which nine were two-seaters. Similarly, along with his four DH 2s, von Richthofen was credited with eight two-seaters and three BE 12s, which had been converted from two-seat BE 2cs into single-seat 'fighters' that were wholly unsuited to aerial combat with an Albatros D I/II.

The RFC pilots had lower total scores, but often had a mixed bag of victories over various single- and two-seat types. For instance, No. 24 Sqn's Patrick Langan-Byrne was credited with ten victories, and his tally included two unknown types, four single-seaters and four two-seaters. D Is and D IIs do not figure prominently in victory scores because the RFC pilots simultaneously faced Halberstadt Ds and Fokker Ds, and if in trouble the Albatros Ds could dive away and escape. Case in point is No. 24 Sqn's Robert Saundby, who in his report of 23 November 1916 stated that after firing on an Albatros it 'suddenly wobbled and dived so steeply with engine on that I could not follow him, although I dived up to 130mph'.

Still, as is true in all aerial combat, if a DH 2 could gain a position of advantage and attack unseen, they could best the Albatros. This was indeed the case with Kirmaier's death, the ace being downed by two DH 2s while he was apparently intent on chasing another aeroplane.

Jasta 9 Albatros D IIs chocked and warming up shortly before takeoff in February 1917. Interestingly, the centre and left machines have been fitted with wheel fenders. (Greg VanWyngarden)

Although the Germans regained air superiority as 1916 waned, in truth the DH 2 had not been slaughtered wholesale. Rather, outnumbered by the reorganised and expanding *Luftstreitkräfte*, and with performance inferior to that of the Albatros, it simply was unable to arrest the tide of German superiority. Although the number of D Is and D IIs shot down by RFC pilots is low, they were involved in the deaths of two *Jasta* 2 *Staffelführer* (both at the hands of No. 24 Sqn DH 2s), and with the demise of Boelcke they issued the *Luftstreitkräfte* one of the worst blows it endured during the entire war. *Jasta* 2 struck back by killing No. 24 Sqn CO Lanoe Hawker – 'the English Boelcke' as von Richthofen described him – and Gerald Knight, who had been involved in the events that led to Boelcke's death, although by the time he was killed he had been transferred to No. 29 Sqn.

In essence, not only were *Jasta* 2 Albatros D Is and D IIs and No. 24 Sqn DH 2s involved in duels, but with their various clashes it can be considered that the entire *Staffel* and squadron were in a duel as well.

Men gather around the shattered and broken remains of *Jasta* 1 Albatros D II D.1757/16, flown by Ltn Gustav Leffers, two days after Christmas 1916. (Greg VanWyngarden)

Jasta 8 pilots stand before an Albatros D I fitted with a radiator expansion tank ahead of the cylinders, rather than the common triangular tank above the engine. It had been believed that this configuration was exclusive to a solitary pre-production D I in *Jasta* 2, but it appears there were at least two pre-production machines so outfitted. (Greg VanWyngarden)

Finished in a striking camouflage, Albatros D II D.1768/16 served as an advanced trainer with *Fliegerersatzabteilungen* 5 (Aviation Replacement Unit, or *FEA* 5) in Hannover, Germany. (Collection DEHLA)

Determining the leading *Jagdstaffelpiloten* DH 2 'killers' while flying an Albatros D I or D II is often problematical due to a paucity of detailed records regarding which make-and-model aeroplanes they flew. For instance, *Jasta* 1 was equipped with Fokker

Leading DH 2 Albatros D I/D II killers (credited victories)

Pilot	Squadron	D I/II	Total
Selden Long	24	3	9
William Curphey	32	3	6
Kelvin Crawford	24	3	5
Eric Pashley	24	2	8
Hubert Jones	32	2	7
John Andrews	24	1	12

Leading Albatros D I/D II DH 2 killers (credited victories)

Pilot	*Jasta*	DH 2s	Total
Manfred von Richthofen	2	4	80
Hans von Keudell	1	3*	12
Otto Bernert	4	2*	27
Dieter Collin	2	2	13
Oswald Boelcke	2	1	40
Erwin Böhme	2	1	24
*Unknown as to whether all DH 2 victories were attained in Albatros D-type			

and Halberstadt Ds, but apparently three pilots might have flown Albatros D Is on 31 August when attacking G 100 Martinsyde 'Elephants' from No. 27 Sqn. Ltns Gustav Leffers and Hans von Keudell and Oblt Hans Bethge received credit for downing Martinsydes, but it is unknown if they achieved these victories specifically while flying Albatros Ds.

A photograph shows *Jasta* 1's Hptm Martin Zander and Oblt Karl von Greiffenhagen with Halberstadt D-types in the background, although it is known that Fw Leopold Reimann brought an Albatros D I with him when he transferred from *Jasta* 1 to *Jasta* 2 at the beginning of September. This provides provenance that *Jasta* 1 had at least one and possibly more Albatros D-types on strength.

Leffers was shot down and killed on 27 December while battling FE 2s, and although it was thought he had been flying a captured Nieuport at the time, No. 11 Sqn claimed an Albatros D II. A photograph of Leffers' crashed machine reveals that it was in fact Albatros D II D.1757/16. Yet the make and model of aeroplane he flew during his four credited victories (one of which was DH 2 7925 from No. 29 Sqn) between 31 August and 9 November is unknown.

Jasta 8 Vzfw Walter Göttsch stands before his white-painted Albatros D II between late autumn 1916 and early winter 1917. Note the extra access panels near the Windhoff radiator, as well as the insulated intake manifold and protective blast trough for the Maxim machine gun. (Lance Bronnenkant)

Similarly, *Jasta* 8 was initially equipped with both Fokker E- and D-types, but again a photograph dated early autumn 1916 shows an Albatros D I in the background. Also, *Jasta* 8 pilot Ltn Walter Göttsch was photographed next to a white Albatros D II, although the date of this shot is not known finitely beyond a window between October 1916 and January 1917. He appears dressed for cold weather, but perhaps it was only to combat the year-round cold at flight altitudes? As of now the date remains unknown, although it is certainly possible that Walter Göttsch flew an Albatros D II when he shot down a No. 29 Sqn DH 2 for his second victory on 17 November 1916.

Other victories are much more finite, such as Boelcke's single DH 2 victory (7873 of No. 24 Sqn) flying Albatros D II D.386/16, or von Richthofen's downing of Hawker and Knight while flying an Albatros D II. Still, even in cases of such clear Albatros-flown victory association, identifying the aircraft's exact make-and-model (D I or D II) or serial number can be nearly impossible. Many pilots occasionally flew machines other than their normal mounts, and frequently photographs reveal that serial numbers were overpainted (e.g. *Jasta* 2) or, in the case of OAW- and LVG-built Albatrosses, absent from the tails altogether. Also, already scarce combat reports often contain very little information regarding the make-and-model of fighter being flown by the aces. For instance, von Richthofen's translated victory claims note his aeroplane's serial number only once during his first 52 victories, when he indicated having flown 'Albatros D.481', a first production batch D II, while attaining his 15th credited victory.

AFTERMATH

The winter of 1916–17 in Western Europe has been described as one of particularly harsh conditions and, quite expectedly, the pace of combat operations slowed for both sides, affording time for self-assessment and strategic planning. The Entente rejected a Central Powers peace proposal that included the annexation of territories they currently occupied, and French dissatisfaction with Gen Joffre's inability to break the Western Front attrition led to his replacement by Gen Robert Nivelle. The latter had fought at Verdun, and believed the success of his artillery-based counterattacks there could be amplified and implemented along the entire front, which would dissolve the two-year deadlock.

To assist with his plan to 'break the enemy's front in such a manner that the rupture can be immediately exploited', Nivelle proposed that British Field Marshal Sir Douglas Haig's forces conduct preparatory attacks at Arras and Bapaume, with Cambrai as the main objective, to draw out German reserves. The French would then launch a major offensive in the Champagne that employed intense artillery fire followed by massive infantry frontal attacks.

However, Gen Ludendorff recognised that Joffre's replacement with the offensive-minded Nivelle meant an offensive was likely to arrive with the spring. Therefore, the German lines, which bulged into enemy territory between Arras and Riems, had to be fortified. Ludendorff duly established a line of defence at the base of this salient called the *Siegfriedstellung* (Siegfried Zone, or 'Hindenburg Line', as it was known by the Allies), which at some points was 20 miles behind the original German lines. In February 1917 the Germans withdrew to this shorter and more readily defended line. The territory they had occupied was abandoned to the Allies, although everything of value had been destroyed, mined or booby-trapped as they went. This withdrawal was completed by 16 March, and it provided the Germans with a heavily fortified line that could be defended by fewer troops than before, with reserve forces positioned in such a way that they could quickly respond to an attack anywhere along the *Siegfriedstellung*.

Meanwhile, the German *Jagdstaffeln* continued their organisation, and although the Albatros D II's presence was still strong, the new Albatros D III began arriving in ever increasing numbers. Redesigned as a sesquiplane with a lower wing of reduced chord that initially suffered from serious structural integrity issues, the fighter had had these problems rectified by February (although D III pilots knew not to prosecute a protracted dive lest they risk departure of a lower wing). This allowed the Germans to swarm the British reconnaissance two-seaters continually sent across the lines to gather intelligence in support of the pending offensive.

The RFC still flew DH 2s in support of these reconnaissance machines and on offensive patrols of their own, but it was now clear that the pushers were well past their prime. New types had been promised, such as the Bristol F 2A and SE 5, but these would not trickle in until April. For the time being, Trenchard had no choice but make do with what he had.

Thus, the stage was set for the German and Entente forces to engage in what has become known as 'Bloody April', particularly as regards the aerial battles associated with the British Arras offensive that began on 9 April. Casualty figures vary, but more than 240 RFC machines were lost to either German aeroplanes or ground fire, with 300+ airmen killed, wounded or missing.

Meanwhile, the ground offensives for which these men perished enjoyed initial success that quickly faded. British forces were unable to prosecute their initial gains

Oblt Robert Greim of *Jasta* 34 aboard Albatros D III D.2108/16. The D III's obvious visual difference from a D I and D II was its reduced chord lower wing that required the interplane struts attach in a 'V' at the single spar. Although the design's initial structural problems in January 1917 were serious, they were rectified well enough by April to permit the D III to inflict enormous casualties upon RFC two-seater reconnaissance aeroplanes.

in the face of strengthened German resistance, and Nivelle's 16 April offensive – employing more than one million men and 7,000 artillery pieces – suffered from lack of surprise, reduced intelligence from the high casualty rate of aerial reconnaissance aeroplanes and strong German counter artillery. Also, the French 'rolling barrage' that employed a curtain of artillery fire ahead of and at the same speed as advancing troops, progressed too rapidly and subjected the soldiers to catastrophic German machine gun fire. The French managed to capture the first German line before they were stopped, but this 600 yard advance fell well short of Nivelle's expected six miles, and in the first five days they had endured 120,000 men killed or wounded.

Overall the offensive was observed as a flagrant waste of human life, and by month-end the survivors began rebelling, refusing to attack any further and agreeing to fight only in defence of the French lines. News of rebellion resounded through the trenches and soon the French army endured widespread mutiny. The entire fiasco led to Nivelle being relieved of command, but at that point even reservists refused to go to the lines. By June, 54 French divisions were mired in mutinies.

Nivelle's successor, Gen Philippe Pétain, ended these mutinies without blanket punishments, for he deemed the soldiers had been involved in 'collective indiscipline' rather than premeditated mutiny. He also acquiesced to their demands for improved rations, medical care and increased leave, and adopted a policy of 'aggressive defence', whereby future French offensives would be of limited and more realistic scope. Toward that end he chose to somewhat bide his time until the Americans – who had declared war on Germany on 6 April 1917 – began arriving in force. Unfortunately, this would not be until well into 1918.

FURTHER READING

BOOKS

Cooksley, P., *de Havilland DH 2 in Action* (SquadronSignal Publications, 1999)

Davis, M., *Airco – The Aircraft Manufacturing Company* (Crowood Press Ltd, 2001)

Franks, N., *Jagdstaffel Boelcke* (Grub Street, 2004)

Gray, B. J., *The AMC DH 2* (Windsock Datafile 48, Albatross Publications, 2009)

Grosz, P. M., *Albatros D I/D II* (Windsock Datafile 100, Albatross Publications, 2003)

Guttman, J., *Osprey Aircraft of the Aces 88 – Pusher Aces of World War 1* (Osprey Publishing, 2009)

Hawker, T. M., *Hawker VC* (Mitre Press, 1965)

Höfling, R., *Albatros D II – Germany's Legendary World War I Fighter* (Schiffer Books, 2002)

Kilduff, P., *The Red Baron* (Doubleday, 1969)

Kilduff, P., *Red Baron – The Life and Death of an Ace* (David & Charles Ltd, 2007)

Lewis, G. H., *Wings Over the Somme 1916–1918* (William Kimber & Co. Ltd, 1976)

McCudden, J., *Flying Fury – Five Years in the Royal Flying Corps* (Greenhill, 2000)

Miller, J. F., *Manfred von Richthofen – The Aircraft, Myths and Accomplishments of 'The Red Baron'* (Air Power Editions, 2009)

Revell, A., *British Single-Seater Fighter Squadrons on the Western Front in World War I* (Schiffer, 2006)

Van Wyngarden, G., *Osprey Aircraft of the Aces 73 – Early German Aces of World War 1* (Osprey Publishing, 2006)

Van Wyngarden, G., *Osprey Aviation Elite Units 26 – Jagdstaffel 2 'Boelcke' – von Richthofen's Mentor* (Osprey Publishing, 2007)

MAGAZINE ARTICLES

Fant, D. V., 'Many Battles and Many a Bold Adventure', *Over the Front*, Vol. 5, No. 1, Spring 1990, pp. 35–52

Gray, B. J., 'The Anatomy of an Aeroplane', *Cross & Cockade International*, Vol. 20, No. 1, 1989, pp. 1–25

Miller, J. F., 'Eight Minutes Near Bapaume', *Over the Front*, Vol. 21, No. 2, Summer 2006, pp. 120–138

INDEX

References to illustrations are shown in **bold**.